Deadly Bribe

The History of a Fritz Sauckel WWII Walther Presentation Pistol

Rudolf E. Kraus

Foreword by Thomas Whiteman, PhD

GREAT BANYAN PRESS

Published by Great Banyan Press

Copyright © 2021 by Rudolf E. Kraus

All rights reserved. No part of this book may be reproduced or transmitted in any form or by any means, electronic or mechanical, including photocopying, recording, or by any information storage and retrieval system, without permission in writing from the author, except for the inclusion of brief quotations in a review.

The Great Banyan Press logo is a trademark of Rudolf E. Kraus.

ISBN: 979-8-5820-7361-1

Cover design by Ellen Meyer and Vicki Lesage

Table of Contents

Foreword i
Introduction 1
A Look at the Subject Walther Model PP 5
History of the Walther PP 13
Background about Fritz Sauckel 15
Commentary on Wilhelm Gustloff 19
Background on the City of Weimar 25
The 1938 Weimar Gautag 31
Sauckel Goes into Hiding 41
The Nuremburg Trial and Sauckel's Botched Execution 43
Possible Recipients: The Long List 47
Military or Civilian? 57
Narrowing the Search: The Short List 63
Photographic Records 77
Wartime Diaries and Private Documents 79
Getting War Booty Home 81
Family Provenance of the Pistol 85
Title and Legal Matters 95
The Question of Valuation 97
Authentication from Letters and Factory Records 105
Postscript 109
APPENDIX A: Serial Numbers of Factory Engraved Walthers
 113
APPENDIX B: The Author's Affinity for Firearms 115
A Note from the Author 119
About the Author 121
Acknowledgments 123
Table of Illustrations 125
References 127

Foreword

FOR OVER 50 YEARS I've been a collector of historic military firearms, from the Civil War through Desert Storm. These firearms represent living history and honor the veterans who fought and died for our freedoms. I've made it my mission to educate others and share the stories behind these artifacts to raise awareness and understanding.

I started collecting vintage firearms in college. Although I had little money, I was fascinated with history, especially military history. The first gun I bought was a Luger. At the time, I was working at a supermarket for $2 an hour. I purchased the pistol for $150 and showed it to my boss, who promptly offered $300 for it. This is when the light bulb went off, and I realized I could buy and sell historical weapons. It was nearly 50 years later that I started Legacy Collectibles. We sell guns throughout the U.S. and related accessories all around the world. Our YouTube channel has over 40,000 subscribers. My hobby is now my business—my dream job.

While I collect firearms from many wars, my particular area of interest is World War II collectible weapons from both sides of the conflict. Fine engraved Nazi-era Walther PPs are my specialty. I'm often asked why I collect Nazi weapons. The short answer is that guns with a history are nearly always connected to war. World War II has been romanticized over the decades as it was the purest war: a true battle of good vs. evil. In this war, the greatest generation sacrificed their lives for a noble cause. It gives me goosebumps every time I think about it.

The Third Reich was big on pomp and ceremony. The German military loved showing off with parades and festivals, badges and awards. Engraved pistols were given on special occasions as ceremonial tokens of thanks. Many people haven't heard of Fritz Sauckel, but he gave away the largest number of ceremonial engraved pistols apart from Heinrich Himmler. It was likely that Sauckel was acquainted with Himmler because Himmler would have used Sauckel's Thüringen connections to get engraved pistols from factories in that district.

These ceremonial handguns are exceedingly rare, with approximately 200 having been manufactured in total. Of those, between 12 and 20 engraved Walther PPs were signed by infamous war criminal Fritz Sauckel. And of those Sauckel PPs, some remain undiscovered. I expect that more will show up over time as attics get cleaned out after WWII GIs pass away.

The engraved pistol that is the subject of this book is one of those rare handguns. This Nazi ceremonial pistol is even more unusual than other Fritz Sauckel presentation Walthers. Not only does it have Sauckel's engraved signature, it also has the date of the Gautag celebration on November 5-6, 1938. To make it even more unique, embedded in the left grip is a medallion containing the recipient's initials.

When I first heard about this project, I admit I rolled my eyes a little. How much can you say about an individual gun? How could an entire book be written about one? But as I read, I realized it was about so much more, including the cronyism of the Nazi party as it grew in power, the internal corruption that I believe would have eventually destroyed the Third Reich, even without WWII. Nazis frequently gifted properties, estates, and businesses

Deadly Bribe

to gain favor within the party. It was extremely important to know the right people. I am reminded of Oskar Schindler, who many may be familiar with from the 1993 film Schindler's List. He did a lot of bribing and general sucking up to get Nazi contracts for his factories. He threw extravagant parties and paid bribes in diamonds, illicit booze, gold, vacations to his villa in Krakow, and other luxury items so that he could gain more workers. Of course the Nazis didn't realize that he then helped save the lives of more than 1,200 Jewish workers. He continued bribing SS officials to prevent the execution of his workers until the end of the war, by which time he had spent his entire fortune on bribes and black market purchases of supplies for his workers.

It's said that "Not all art is in frames" and that's certainly true about engraved firearms. Fritz Sauckel engraved pistols are beautiful works of art. Despite its sinister past, the Walther PP described in this book is truly an elegant handgun. The Walther company was well-known for its high quality and beautiful firearms. While we may abhor the history of the Nazi regime, we can still marvel at the workmanship and beauty of this piece.

This pistol is entwined with history in many ways. First of course is its donor—the notorious Fritz Sauckel. Second is its presentation during an important Nazi ceremony, attended by Adolf Hitler himself. And thirdly, the recipient of the pistol, while still unproven, was likely a Nazi judge. The author, Rudy Kraus, proposes a theory with a conclusion that is logical and provides a compelling argument. The judge had a lot of influence within the Nazi party, and this would have been a well-placed bribe.

I watch a lot of documentaries about WWII, read books about WWII, and generally consider myself well-informed about its history—and even I learned new things from this book. I'm sure you'll enjoy this easy-to-read and informative book, about a lot more than a gun. As the president and founder of Legacy Collectibles, I've seen many historic weapons over the years, but few have the fascinating history of this one. Sit back and enjoy the ride as Rudy takes you along on his journey to identify the recipient. Read about the remarkable history of this unique handgun and its place in World War II history.

Tom Whiteman, 2021

Introduction

AMERICANS HAVE A LONGSTANDING AFFINITY for nostalgic firearms. Hollywood has certainly intensified this attraction with depictions of western bad guys and good guys, 007, war heroes, Dirty Harry, Bonnie and Clyde, and dozens more.

For the serious collector, the pinnacle of acquisition is a firearm associated with a famous event or historic person. Firearms are mere tools; tools employed by those on both sides of the law. Some firearms are attributed to notorious outlaws.

In this book I recount the story behind one such firearm: what I call the Fritz Sauckel Walther Presentation Pistol. This pistol is tied to not one but several infamous criminals. The story involves evil that is almost unimaginable. The death toll numbers in the hundreds of thousands.

This historic pistol was given by Ernst "Fritz" Sauckel, a war criminal, to an important Nazi official at a festival attended by Adolf Hitler. Herein I provide the provenance of the firearm as well as background information about Nazi Germany and the key Nazis involved with the pistol. I detail my journey to identify the mysterious recipient of the ceremonial pistol. My intent is to convince you—the reader—of the authenticity and value of the pistol based on its condition and historical significance.

The magnitude of evil associated with this Walther Model PP is massive. At Sauckel's trial at Nuremburg, he admitted to an estimated five million forced workers placed in German factories. Conditions in these labor camps were harsh and cruel. An estimated one million of these workers perished. The toll of evil does not stop there. In this story I demonstrate ties to Kristallnacht, the horrific night that led to the Holocaust, resulting in the murder of six million Jews.

Few firearms exist that can even come close to matching this evil. This story isn't pretty, but I believe it needs to be told. And why should it be told by me?

Because I'm the firearm's current owner.

My father purchased the pistol in 1953, and it has been in the Kraus family since then. Pop never spoke in any detail of whom he purchased it from but only said that he got it from a guy in Ohio while on a business trip.

Symbolism and ritual were very important to the Nazi party. Torch-lit processions with tens of thousands of people bearing banners were one way they demonstrated their power. Nazis also created many awards and decorations for military, political, and civilian recognition. The presentation of elegant engraved weapons was one such custom of recognition. I estimate that as many as several hundred engraved pistols were presented over the reign of the Third Reich to various dignitaries and Nazi "big shots." In many cases, a pistol might be given as thanks for faithful service, but I believe Fritz Sauckel presented this pistol as a bribe, an inducement for a future favor. This bribe turned out to be deadly.

Of course, not all presentation pieces have survived or surfaced. Some of them, such as a number of engraved presentation pistols ordered by Heinrich Himmler, were still in the manufacturing stages at the end of the war. American forces liberated these as war booty at the factory. They were never finished and thus never presented to the intended recipients. Yet others were mutilated at war's end, usually by physically grinding off identification marks so as to obscure the identity. Such mutilation was not uncommon. The recipients—high-ranking Nazis—were subject to likely prosecution for war crimes following the capitulation of Germany. Those high-ranking Nazis were running for cover as the Third Reich imploded and hence were prone to destroying, burying, or hiding any incriminating evidence that could be later used against them in war crimes trials.

My pistol is therefore very rare for surviving unscathed. Now it is time for the pistol to tell its tale: what are its origins and who was its intended recipient?

A Look at the Subject Walther Model PP

THIS STORY CENTERS AROUND a rather unusual nickel-plated and oak leaf engraved Walther Model PP pistol. The firearm is a 7.65 mm caliber (.32 auto). It has gold dust inlay and ivory grips. Embedded in the left grip is a recipient medallion. There is a crown N proof mark on the slide. The date inscribed is 5-6. XI. 1938. The serial number is 109825P.

The Fritz Sauckel Presentation Walther, view of engraved side

The engraved inscription reads "Von der Wilhelm-Gustloff Stiftung – zum 5-6. XI. 1938." This identifies the pistol as a Wilhelm Gustloff Stiftung presentation piece, presented on November 5-6, 1938. The Roman numeral XI indicates the eleventh month. In the mid-1930s, the NSDAP (Nationalsozialistische Deutsche Arbeiterpartei, translated as National Socialist German Workers' Party, or Nazis) nationalized a number of formerly Jewish-owned armament factories. The group of factories was renamed in tribute to recently assassinated Wilhelm Gustloff (considered a martyr to the Nazis), thus the name *Wilhelm Gustloff Stiftung* (Stiftung meaning association or foundation). Later, in 1940, the name was changed to Gustloffwerkes.

The Wilhelm Gustloff Stiftung engraving

Below the Stiftung inscription is the engraved signature of well-known Nazi war criminal Fritz Sauckel (hanged October 16, 1946 at Nuremberg).

The Fritz Sauckel engraving

Deadly Bribe

Among his numerous other titles, Sauckel was the head of the Wilhelm Gustloff Stiftung, hence his engraved signature as the donor on behalf of the Wilhelm Gustloff Stiftung (Foundation).

The signature has been verified as Fritz (Ernst) Sauckel.

It was common Nazi protocol that the decorated and engraved pistols that high-ranking officials were honored with were of a smaller size and caliber, being ceremonial in nature. The elegant Walther Model PP in 7.65 mm was typical. This cartridge is equivalent to the .32 ACP (Automatic Colt Pistol) cartridge in the U.S. In contrast, most Nazi military were issued larger pistols in 9 mm Parabellum. The most common combat pistols were the Luger, the P38, and the Radom VIS.

The Walther Model PP has to be considered one of the most elegant firearms in its day. Personally, I've always been attracted to the Walther Model PP and Model PPK pistols. The discreet exposed hammer and double action are design features that I rate highly.

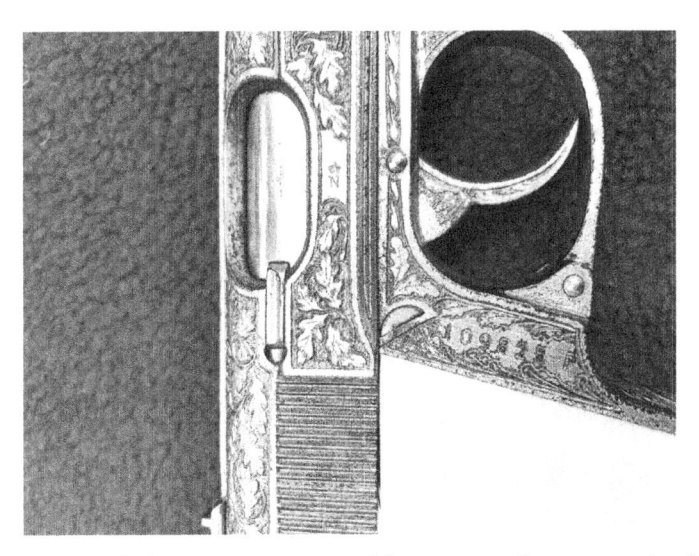

The Fritz Sauckel Presentation Walther, view of reverse side showing the Crown N proof mark and serial number

I confess that I'm far from an expert on the minutiae concerning technical specifications of Nazi era handguns, but I do realize that Walther Model PP pistols were produced with two different variations on the safety lever. These are commonly referred to as 90-degree and 60-degree safety levers. This subject Walther Model PP has the 60-degree configuration. I am also told that the proof marks are critical in determining authenticity and dating. This firearm's slide bears the "Crown N" proof mark.

The left side grip medallion is engraved with the initials "W.B." in Gothic lettering. The medallion is mounted within the ivory grip.

The engraved initials of the recipient on the ivory grip

Nazi custom was to inscribe the recipient's initials on the pistol's grip. For many prominent Nazis, including even Hitler, the initials were carved directly into the ivory grip(s). In the case of the subject Walther, the initials are within an elaborate medallion. I consider this distinction to be significant. The use of the script Gothic initials was indicative of a presentation to a civilian, obviously high-ranking, as opposed to a military recipient. My sense is that Sauckel went to considerable effort to honor the recipient. As such, I view this subject Walther as being in a class above most.

Some might question if the initials are possibly reversed and thus representative of "B.W." I strongly reject the B.W. hypothesis on several grounds:

In studying the frequency of surnames and given names in the German language, I've noted that relatively few first names begin with the letter B, whereas first names with W are very common. For example, Werner, Wilhelm, Walter, Walther, Wolf, and Wolfgang are commonplace.

The listing of names of prominent Nazis in the book *Who's Who in Nazi Germany* by Robert S. Wistrick [1] reveals zero entries of persons with the initials B.W., whereas names with initials W.B. do appear.

When one examines the initials in the above photograph of the medallion, the B appears as the dominant letter, with the W being secondary. As such, I assert that the B represents the recipient's last initial, that being the most important initial.

Consequently, I am of the view that the likelihood of the initials being "B.W." is small, hence my conviction that "W.B." is correct.

I wish to comment on the significance of the magazine. When German forces surrendered at war's end, they were required to give up their arms and ammunition. The bolts were removed from Mauser rifles. Rifles were then placed in piles without the bolts, and the rifle bolts were placed in separate piles. I assume that ammunition was also placed apart. The point is that most arms did not retain all parts. However, the magazine with its engraved flush bottom and gold wash is still with the subject Model PP.

The engraved flush bottom of the magazine, shown slightly extended

Officers and high-ranking Nazis, upon surrender, would customarily hand over their sidearm. Clearly, the subject Model PP was either surrendered or was found intact. The fact that the original magazine is still with the pistol suggests that it was surrendered intact. A second possibility is that a GI found the pistol, perhaps in the quarters of some Nazi big shot. However, I discount that possibility, as the leather holster and second magazine would have been kept with the pistol. Given that the pistol has just one magazine suggests that it was given over during the act of surrender.

The date of manufacture of the subject Model PP remains somewhat obscure. All production records from the factory in Thuringia (the original Walther factory in Zella-Mehlis, near Suhl) that produced the Walther presentation pistols were lost. Bombing of Nazi arms factories destroyed numerous buildings, along with any production records contained within. To compound matters, the retreating German forces destroyed all remaining factory production records. The objective was to obscure the identities of Nazi recipients. It is said that the son of the factory owner was able to flee to the west at war's end with a briefcase filled with technical drawings, but the production records did not survive. Those technical drawings later permitted the company to come back to life, post war. It's likely that a number of Walther Model PP's were selected for presentation pieces at the Zella-Mehlis factory. The engraving at the factory was usually done prior to heat treatment and hardening of the metal components. Any engraving after hardening was shallower, and thus easily identified. The deep engraving on this subject Walther PP attests to its authenticity. See Appendix A: Serial Numbers of Factory Engraved Walthers for a list of serial number ranges for these presentation pistols.

View of name of factory where the pistol was produced, Walther Zella-Mehlis

The subject Walther Model PP has the "P" suffix in its serial number. This is consistent with a manufacture date circa 1938. Earlier Model PP Walther pistols had purely numbers. The "P" suffix was introduced to define a new serial numbering range and to prevent the need for going into the millions.

Because the Third Reich in the 1930s was violating the terms of the Treaty of Versailles, arms manufacturers adopted intentionally confusing serial numbering practices to mislead the inspectors. The clear objective was to mask the degree to which Germany was rearming. Therefore, it's a mistake to assume a string of consecutively numbered firearms.

History of the Walther PP

CARL WALTHER STARTED HIS OWN RIFLE-MAKING BUSINESS in 1886, although the Walther family had been in the gun manufacturing business since the 1700s. He built a small factory in Zella-Mehlis in 1903. Carl's son Fritz convinced him to turn to semi-automatic pistols, and in 1908 they produced their first prototype, the Model 1. Fritz recognized the potential of the double-action revolver technology and incorporated it into his latest model in 1929, introducing the Walther PP.

The Walther PP is a compact, powerful, and reliable weapon. It was originally issued to German police, hence the PP (Polizei Pistole or Police Pistol). As the first commercially successful double-action semi-automatic pistol, it occupies a significant place in firearms history. The Walther operates on a straight blowback system with a double/single action—a double-action trigger pull for the first shot, and a lighter single-action pull for follow-up shots. This set the standard for double-action pistol manufacturers that's been in effect worldwide for the past 90 years.

The PP was chambered for 7.65 mm (.32 ACP) cartridges, with a magazine capacity of 8 rounds. It weighs 1.5 pounds and is 6.8 inches long. Although some models were chambered for .380 ACP ammunition, the 7.65 was the only ceremonial model.

Because it performed so well, the German army adopted it for Panzer crews, Luftwaffe pilots, and Wehrmacht officers. Due to its popularity with both sides during the war, as well as its admirable performance, production of the Walther PP continued after the war.

The PPK (Polizei Pistole Kriminalmodell, or Police Pistol Detective Model) variation was introduced a few months after the PP. Some sources say the "K" stands for "kurz," the German word for short, as this model is about a half inch shorter than the PP. It was designed for undercover use and had a shorter barrel, frame, and grip. Like the PP, it was used by officers and pilots during the war.

The PPK became famous in the early 1960s when it was adopted as the main sidearm of fictional British spy James Bond. Author Ian Fleming featured a .25 Auto Beretta in his novel *Casino Royale* as Bond's main handgun, but was informed by Geoffrey Boothroyd, a retired Army Major and gun collector, that the Beretta was not powerful enough for the job, so Fleming replaced it with the PPK.

Background about Fritz Sauckel

FRITZ SAUCKEL, the donor of the subject pistol, was the only child of a postman and a seamstress. At the age of 15, he dropped out of high school and joined the merchant marines of Norway and Sweden. His ship was captured at the beginning of World War I, and he was held prisoner for five years. After the war, Sauckel lived in poverty as an unskilled worker, for which he blamed the Jews.

He was an early member of the Nazi party, joining in 1923 with party number 1395. In 1927, he was appointed Gauleiter, or provincial party leader, of Thuringia (Thüringen). He received the honorary rank of Obergruppenführer in the Sturmabteilung (SA), a Nazi militia notorious for its violence and terrorism, in 1933. In 1942, Sauckel was appointed the first Generalbevollmächtigter für den Arbeitseinsatz (General Plenipotentiary for the Employment of Labor) by Martin Bormann.

In this position, Sauckel imported 4,800,000 workers from the Soviet Union and Poland to work in German factories during the war. He forced Polish workers to wear a letter "P" patch to distinguish them from Germans. Most were taken by force to the Reich. Conditions for the workers were extremely harsh, with starvation rations barely keeping them alive. Discipline was severe. Sauckel's attitude toward these laborers was expressed in a letter to Alfred Rosenberg, the head of the NSDAP Office of Foreign Affairs, on April 20, 1942, where he wrote, "All the men must be fed, sheltered, and treated in such a way as to exploit them to the highest possible extent at the lowest conceivable degree of expenditure."

The most common photograph of Ernst "Fritz" Sauckel

In 1946, he was one of 24 major war criminals accused in the Nuremberg Trial before the International Military Tribunal. He was found guilty of war crimes and crimes against humanity, and sentenced to death by hanging. Surprised by the announcement of his death sentence, Sauckel burst into tears and blamed translation errors of his statements as the cause.

In his private diary, Joseph Goebbels called Sauckel, "...a short, stolid man with a bald head and a minimal toothbrush mustache." Historian Joseph Persico described him as "...a little man with a shining dome, sad brown eyes, and a silly moustache patterned after the Führer's."

Fritz Sauckel (1894-1946)

In both of the photos above of Fritz Sauckel in military uniform, his rank insignia are that of an SS (Schutzstaffel) Oberführer, equivalent to a Brigadier General.

This ornate Walther (below) is alleged to have been Sauckel's personal pistol. Its poor condition resulted from having been buried for decades until later being dug up and retrieved by his family. Many Nazi-era presentation pieces suffered equal or worse outcomes. Note the 90-degree safety lever configuration.

Sauckel's personal pistol

Another observation is that the owners (recipients) were sometimes identified by their initials on the grip and other times by their name engraved onto the piece. Note even Fritz Sauckel's own firearm shows only his initials. I will return to the topic of engraved name vs. initials, and so I wish to point out the distinction now. It is my understanding that even Adolf Hitler's sidearm bore only his initials.

Fritz Sauckel met his end in Nuremburg at the hands of Master Sergeant John C. Woods, hangman.

Commentary on Wilhelm Gustloff

BECAUSE THE SUBJECT MODEL PP WAS GIVEN under the name of the *Wilhelm Gustloff Stiftung*, it is appropriate to provide some commentary on Wilhelm Gustloff himself (January 30, 1895 – February 4, 1936). Gustloff, the Gauleiter of the Nazis in Switzerland, was assassinated in his Swiss apartment by David Frankfurter, a Jewish medical student from Croatia. After the assassination, Frankfurter surrendered to Swiss police.

In addition to being the head of the Nazi party in Switzerland, Gustloff was a close friend of Hitler. Frankfurter's act of assassinating Gustloff was, in general, not repulsive to the Swiss populace, but nonetheless murder is murder. Under Swiss law, the assassin was tried and sentenced to prison for 18 years. Some sources say that Frankfurter was sentenced to life. He was released after serving nine years. Following his release in the fall of 1945, David Frankfurter moved to (or was exiled to) Israel.

Shown on the next page is a Nazi propaganda poster following Gustloff's assassination. Frankfurter is in the lower right with the description "The Murderer." Gustloff's photo in his Nazi uniform is in the upper left.

Gustloff assassination Nazi propaganda poster

In making a martyr out of Wilhelm Gustloff for the Nazis, two major entities were given his name within the Third Reich.

(1) **The Wilhelm Gustloff Stiftung,** which took over control of former Jewish-owned ("aryanized") armament factories. Fritz Sauckel was the head of that effort. The former Simson factory in Weimar that produced many of Germany's small arms became known as the Fritz Sauckel Werke (as part of the larger Gustloff umbrella).

(2) The large luxury German ocean liner, the *M.S. Wilhelm Gustloff*, was launched May 5, 1937.

[Note: In the below discussion of the ship, these details have no bearing on the subject Walther Model PP, however I found the topic so interesting that I have nonetheless included it.]

The *M.S. Wilhelm Gustloff* was already under construction when Gustloff was assassinated in 1936. The ship's name was then changed from the intended *M.S. Adolf Hitler* to that of *M.S. Wilhelm Gustloff*. This ship is a story in itself as it was a "Strength Through Joy" luxury liner. The ship was used before the outbreak of the war to provide Atlantic and Baltic cruise vacations for Third Reich workers as a reward for their hard work. When World War

II broke out on September 1, 1939, the *M.S. Wilhelm Gustloff* was converted for use as a hospital ship.

The M.S. Wilhelm Gustloff painted white as a hospital ship

In November 1940, the *M.S. Wilhelm Gustloff* was again changed in use, this time to a docked barracks for housing German naval personnel. The docked ship was relatively immune from bombing as it was so far east in the Baltic, beyond the normal reach of Allied planes based in England.

In late January 1945, the *M.S. Wilhelm Gustloff* was hastily made seaworthy at the Baltic port of Gotenhafen (near Danzig) and was loaded in a desperate effort with an estimated 10,000 or more Germans fleeing to escape the Red Army approaching from the east. This passage, its final passage it turns out, required that the ship be reactivated after having been unused for over four years. Among the passengers were approximately 1,000 trained Nazi submarine crew members seeking to return to U-boat duties to destroy Allied shipping. The list of passengers also included as many as 4,000 children.

At about 9 PM on the night of January 30, 1945, the *M.S. Wilhelm Gustloff* was squarely hit by three torpedoes from the Soviet Submarine S-13, causing the vessel to sink within 45 minutes. A story titled *Crabwalk* was later written by a man named Gunter Grass, and it detailed the events of the *M.S. Wilhelm Gustloff* and its sinking. Based on Internet scans, it seems that the title *Crabwalk* refers to a process of looking forward (to the future) by scuttling backwards, thus using history as a way to look forward. As incredible as this may sound, Gunter Grass was born that very night at sea to an unwed mother, a passenger on the *M.S. Wilhelm Gustloff*, just after being saved by a rescue vessel.

As to the sinking, the Soviet submarine was faster than the former ocean liner because it was running on the surface unlighted at night under diesel power as opposed to batteries. The *M.S. Wilhelm Gustloff* was running with its night navigation lights turned on, as its Captain felt there was minimal risk of attack at that point since it was close to its intended port, Kiel, in mainland Germany.

Matters on board the lighted *M.S. Wilhelm Gustloff* were also complicated by the presence of the Nazi U-Boat submarine crews, including four submarine commanders. It has been suggested that the four commanders were throwing their weight and opinions around causing bickering and arguments, thus adding to the confusion. The faster submarine S-13 was able to easily track the *M.S. Wilhelm Gustloff* and position itself for direct broadside hits. Most of the ship's lifeboats couldn't be used because ice covered the davits, the cranes used for lowering lifeboats, and maintenance on the davits (I assume) had been neglected for the years at dockside.

An estimated 9,400 lives were lost in the icy Baltic waters, or about six times the number lost in the sinking of the *Titanic*. This catastrophe remains the greatest maritime loss of all time, and yet the news of the *M.S. Wilhelm Gustloff's* sinking was barely covered in any newspapers, neither inside Germany nor outside Germany. Bear in mind that this ship was built as a peacetime luxury ocean liner, and not according to military standards. Three torpedoes aimed broadside were sufficient to doom the ship and most aboard. Relatively few survived. The icy Baltic waters in January of 1945 didn't afford a long lifespan for its passengers upon being cast into the sea.

The sinking of the M.S. Wilhelm Gustloff by artist Irwin J. Kappes

An interesting aspect of the military drama that unfolded concerned the status of the Soviet submarine commander. It seems that he was in a situation of disgrace, facing possible court martial or military trial upon return to port. But after sinking the *M.S. Wilhelm Gustloff*, it appears his stature was rectified to becoming a hero of the Soviet Union. While the Nazis could manufacture more U-Boats, the loss of the 1,000 trained men on board the *M.S. Wilhelm Gustloff* certainly worked against their cause.

Background on the City of Weimar

THE NAZI PARTY ADMINISTRATION was divided into many levels: *Reich* (national), *Gau* (state, region, or province), *Kreis* (district or county), *Orts* (town or city), *Zelle* (cell), and *Block* (block). There were 43 Gaus. See the map below. Thuringia (or Thüringen) was one such Gau, with Weimar as its capital city.

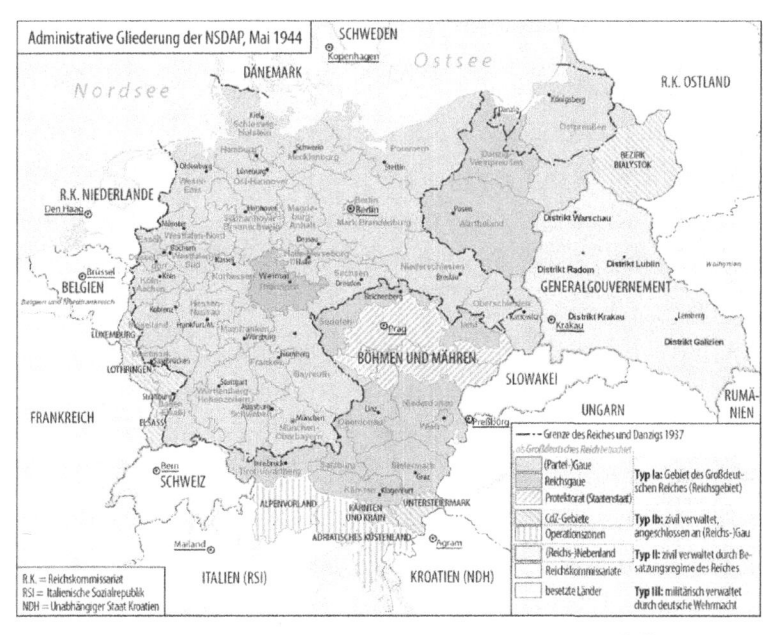

Administrative map of the Third Reich [2]

Fritz Sauckel was appointed as the Gauleiter of Thuringia circa 1927 (possibly 1925, as I have seen two different citations), and then was elevated to Governor of Thuringia in 1933. Sauckel held both positions until the war's end in 1945.

Weimar was the location of the Fritz Sauckel Werke, which was a part of the larger Wilhelm Gustloff Stiftung. Later, in 1940, the name was changed to Gustloffwerkes. Fritz Sauckel was the overall head of the Gustloffwerkes.

The Gustloffwerkes consisted of a number of factories (primarily of Jewish ownership before the Nazis nationalized them). Each factory was associated with a code that was marked on the barrel of the firearms produced there to identify the place of manufacture. These factories were: the Fritz Sauckel Werke in Weimar (code "bcd"); Arms Werke in Suhl (code "dbf"); Meiningen (code "nyw"); Otto Eberhardt Cartridge Factory in Hirtenberg, Austria; Muselwitz Engineering Factory; and a head office in Berlin. The Fritz Sauckel arms factory (the former Simson & Company factory) was large, and it turned out large quantities of small arms, including military Mauser rifles and replacement barrels for tanks.

Weimar was the location of an infamous forced labor camp, Buchenwald. The Buchenwald camp also had an arms factory that the Allies bombed out of production in 1944. Slave and captive labor were used at both the Gustloffwerkes (also called the Fritz Sauckel Werkes), and at the nearby Buchenwald death camp factory.

Buchenwald opened for its first prisoners in 1937. The initial inmates were political prisoners and other undesirables such as Gypsies and Jehovah's Witnesses. The Jews, in contrast, were shipped east to other camps, such as the Auschwitz extermination camp in Poland. Buchenwald was used mostly for housing and supplying slave laborers, who were worked to death nonetheless on a calculated basis of minimal nutrition, hard labor, and exposure. Those who died were replaced with more laborers from the east as the war continued.

About 250,000 prisoners were at Buchenwald at various times, and 50,000 are said to have been executed or worked to death. Bodies were disposed of in the camp's crematorium. Conditions were harsh. Laborers often arrived wearing only one set of clothes, which they slept in and worked in. At times, some had no shoes and yet had to march in the winter conditions and work with no shoes on.

The Buchenwald prison camp was especially cruel, as the Camp Commander's wife, Frau Ilse Koch, had a perversion wherein she liked tattoos. She arranged to have prisoners with tattoos executed and skinned, and then the skin was used to make lampshades and similar artifacts to adorn her house. Frau Ilse Koch was tried and sentenced to life imprisonment in 1951.

In the interests of brevity as well as keeping this document non-gruesome, I have refrained from including photos from the death camps, ovens, etc.

Final aircraft assembly [3]

Nearby caves from mining operations were converted for use as underground factories. The Nazis moved machinery into these underground factories, administered under the banner of the Gustloffwerkes, after the conventional above-ground factories were bombed by the Allies. Underground Gustloff Werke factories near Weimar were used to make jet engines, some jet airplanes, and V-1 and V-2 rockets that took a toll on London at the close of the war.

Bunker 0 of the underground Gustloff Werke factory at Weimar

Bunker 0, shown in the photo above, was built against the hillside. It covered the main tunnels 34 and 35 and was the location of final aircraft assembly, as seen in the 1945 photo below. The side entrance to Bunker 0 was closed by a set of huge sliding doors. *(U.S. National Archives, RG 111-SC).*

The most ambitious Third Reich public building project in Weimar was the Gauforum, north of the city center. During the Third Reich this was known as "Adolf Hitler Platz," under the East Germans as "Karl Marx Platz," and now as "Platz des Friedens" (Peace Square).

Artist's conception of the completed Gauforum

Similar complexes were planned in many German cities, but few were started and fewer still were completed to the level of the Weimar Gauforum (which was, indeed, never completed to plan). The photo above is an artist's conception of the completed Gauforum. The large community hall at the left was never built.

Groundbreaking for the Gauforum May 1, 1937

Construction of the impressive Gauforum building and government complex commenced in Weimar on May 1, 1937. The photo above shows Sauckel turning the first pile of dirt in a groundbreaking ceremony with thousands watching, including Herr Hitler and his entourage. The girls, members of a girl's youth organization, *Bund Deutscher Madel*, are seen in white short sleeves. Their role included strewing flowers before the Führer [4]. Rudolph Hess played a role as well, as I believe that Hess is shown standing just to the right of Hitler.

Approximately forty similar governmental centers were planned throughout Germany, but few other than the center at Weimar were completed. A similar Gauforum was scheduled for construction in Dresden. Hitler had an affinity for planning and overseeing building projects, so he was frequently photographed inspecting replica models and attending groundbreaking ceremonies.

Massive crowds gathered for the speech at the groundbreaking of the Gauforum site [5]

The groundbreaking itself was just one part of the event; around 40,000 persons gathered in the streets of Weimar on May 1, 1937 to celebrate the renaming of the Gauforum site—then named to be the Adolf Hitler Platz.

The 1938 Weimar Gautag

As the Nazi party rose in Germany in the 1920s, annual celebrations in each Gau became customary. The word Gautag translates roughly as "Provincial Party Day." This was like a small version of the National *Reichsparteitag*. The event was used for military parades, speeches, promoting the party, and also as a fundraising mechanism. Flags were flown in abundance, and with much regalia. Funds were raised by the issuance of medallions. It was expected that the loyal Germans would purchase their commemorative medals and proudly wear them.

Postcard from 1938 Weimar Gautag

As a note, the above image of a printed badge for the Weimar Gautag of 1938 was downloaded from an Internet source. The whited out areas were done so as to comply with current laws in the country of origin that prohibit the posting or publication of Nazi emblems.

I have located several photographs of the crowds and parading soldiers at the 1938 Gautag in Weimar. See one such photograph below. The magnitude of the crowd is almost indescribable.

Hitler speaking before a huge crowd at the 1938 Weimar Gautag

The Gautag in Weimar was an especially important one, as Weimar was one of the few cities that allowed the Nazis to assemble in the 1920s, and thus provided Hitler an opportunity to speak in public. The granddaddy of all Gautags first took place in Weimar in 1926; the 1938 Gautag celebrated the 12th anniversary of the first Gautag when Hitler spoke.

Weimar is an ancient German city, dating back as early as 900 AD, and was the government seat of the Thuringia region, an industrial center. Adolf Hitler had a strong interest in Weimar. He traveled to and from the 1938 Gautag by private train. For more information about the details of the events in Weimar, I recommend the book *Weimar im Banne des Führers* by Holm Kirsten [6]. See page 68 of the reference for the events in Weimar (written in German).

Herr Adolf Hitler gave a speech in Weimar on Sunday, November 6, 1938, which coincides with the date of the presentation of the subject ceremonial Walther PP firearm. Although some sources cite Hitler's Weimar speech taking place on November 5, most credible sources confirm that the speech was given by Hitler at 3 PM on Sunday, November 6, 1938. Both dates coincide with the 1938 Weimar Gautag. This demonstrates Hitler's connection with the Sauckel Walther piece. The Hitler speech (as translated) is available online [7].

Hitler and his entourage in Weimar at the 1938 Gautag

The above photograph came from a period newspaper.

At the time of the Weimar Gautag, significant events were transpiring within Germany and elsewhere. One such event just prior to Hitler's Weimar speech was the incorporation of the Sudeten German Heimatfront into the National Socialist party on November 5, 1938. Hitler's speech at Weimar was mostly devoted to bolstering the Sudeten gains as legitimate, while also attacking Britain's Winston Churchill, the minority leader in Britain.

In October of 1938, Churchill had denounced the Sudeten German Heimatfront takeover in Austria in a speech called "A Total and Unmitigated Defeat." During a debate in the House of Commons, Churchill vehemently opposed the strategy of appeasement that Prime Minister Neville Chamberlain advocated towards Hitler, viewing it as a sign of weakness. He warned that if Hitler were not stopped, he would begin planning to take over western Europe. Churchill advocated a buildup of national defenses, arguing that Germany and Hitler were arming for war and had to be stopped immediately.

Hitler used this opportunity at the Gautag to fire back in oratory at Churchill, labeling him a warmonger. And so Weimar became the place in history where Hitler gave his famous rebuttal speech against Churchill. This well-documented history further confirms Hitler's association with the presentation of the subject Walther PP.

Concerning the events of the 1938 Gautag in Weimar, a noted WWII firearms collector wrote to me:

"Gautag Weimar was scheduled to be held earlier in the year, but two factors delayed the event. One was the beginning of the construction of the Gauforum in Weimar and the second was the remodeling of the Hotel Elephant, Hitler's favorite place when visiting Weimar. Earlier in the year, the groundbreaking for the Gauforum occurred. This must be the photo that you found on the net. Hitler also worked with the hotel management by offering remodeling suggestions for his favorite hotel.

"In any case, the hotel was finished by the time of the Gautag Thüringen that took place November 5-6, 1938. There is an online review of a German language book detailing Hitler's speeches. One of the sections provided in the review is that portion of the book dealing with Hitler in Weimar for the Gautag. His itinerary is provided. The references used by the author of the book cite period newspapers describing the event.

"Special honor guests began arriving in Weimar on November 4th. Hitler's private train arrived at 11 AM on the 5th. He was accompanied by Himmler, Bormann, and Speer among those mentioned. He was greeted by thousands and reviewed elements of NSDAP organizations at the train station. His convoy left the train station and headed to the Hotel Elephant by way of the Gauforum construction site. At 3 PM Sauckel opened a reception that was held in the Weisser Saal of the Weimar Schloss. The evening ended with dinner and the opera Aida at the national theater.

"On the 6th, there were two major rallies for Hitler after he signed the Golden Book of the City of Weimar in the late morning. At noon, a parade was held on the Karlsplatz with the observation podium across from the post office. At 3 PM, a huge rally was held at the Landeskampfbahn, the large field to the west of city center, where Hitler gave his famous anti-Churchill speech. Hitler left (Weimar) after the speech by train."

Hitler at Haus Elephant in 1936

The above photograph of Hitler looking out of the second-floor balcony window of "Haus Elephant" was taken on July 3, 1936 (prior to its demolition and rebuilding). Hitler had his own private accommodations where only he used the rooms devoted to him.

In 1937, a decision was made to renovate the Elephant Hotel, so it was closed for complete demolition and was then rebuilt from the ground up. This rebuilding took place between 1937 until late in 1938. It seems that the date for the 1938 Weimar Gautag was pushed back two weeks as the hotel was not ready to open for the originally planned October 22-23, 1938 date.

Hitler at the balcony of the renovated Haus Elephant in November 1938

I found the following commentary regarding the Elephant Hotel on the Internet. It must be a translation, and poor at that, so I have inserted some editing remarks in brackets.

"Thomas Mann set his novel *Lotte in Weimar: The Beloved Returns* [in Weimar, and thus] the old Hotel Elephant is a literary monument. There is not any more. For alleged disrepair, the Hotel Elephant in 1937 [was] torn down to the ground and replaced by a new building. The contract was awarded [to] Hermann Giesler, who was an architect of [the] Adolf Hitler Gauforum in special favor. The Elephant should be the most modern hotel of its time. The use of marble and precious German woods underlined [its] representative character. The popular restaurant [with] elephants in the vaulted cellar of the house was designed according to old Germanic forms. The balcony to the front office was also to become the speaker's platform, highlighted by architectural flagpoles and the relief of the imperial eagle. The garden was in the 1st floor a suite designed for the individual needs of Adolf Hitler, which was not used by other hotel guests. Hitler's birthday was celebrated in 1938 topping the Gautag in November, [as] the [Elephant] house was [then finally] ready for Hitler and his first guest(s)."

The suggestion above that Hitler celebrated his birthday in November 1938 is confusing at best. Hitler's actual birthday was April 20, 1889. Moreover, Hitler's 50th birthday on April 20, 1939 was a massive national holiday complete with many festivities. My only guess is that the original scheduled date of the Gautag in October would have coincided with Hitler's half-year birthday. Nonetheless, the re-opening of the Elephant Hotel in November 1938 must have been a cause for much festivity.

To help pay the cost of holding the event, and to generally fatten the Nazi party coffers, it was common practice to create a badge commemorating the day and sell the badges for a small amount to visitors. The badges were bought by virtually everyone attending and were worn during the Gautag event to show support for the party. At the end of the day many people kept the badges as a remembrance. Today collectors commonly refer to these types of badges as "tinnies." This late change in the date of the Weimar Gautag caused some of the tinnies to be produced with the wrong date, as some of the available tinnies show a date of October 22-23, 1938.

Weimar Gautag tinnie with incorrect date

The tinnie shown above is from a recent Internet listing. The tinnie is about the same size as an American half-dollar piece. It has a clip on the reverse side so it can be pinned to clothing. The date of October 22-23 was changed to two weeks later, but the tinnies already manufactured were issued nonetheless bearing the incorrect date.

The change of the date of the Weimar Gautag from October 22-23 to November 5-6 of 1938 impacted the subject Walther Model PP presentation piece. Because the date is inscribed correctly on the Sauckel Walther, this means that the decision to do the engraving was made after the postponement of the Gautag had been finalized. A second observation is that the date on the subject Sauckel Walther is actually two dates, being November 5 and November 6, 1938. This further supports the contention that the Sauckel Walther was given as a commemorative piece coinciding with the events of the two-day-long Weimar Gautag.

It stands to reason that the presentation of the engraved Walther piece by Sauckel in Weimar was a planned event, as the engraving was obviously ordered in advance and without foreknowledge of the Sudeten German Heimatfront aggressive actions by the NSDAP which happened to coincide. As the events of those two days unfolded, they were in part planned and in part impromptu spurred by the unfolding of world events.

Sauckel Goes into Hiding

AS GERMANY IMPLODED at the close of WWII, Fritz Sauckel went into hiding. Sauckel took refuge within the network of caves and underground bunkers in Thuringia as he had access and intimate knowledge of the layout, stashed resources, and people who could help him hide. Fritz Sauckel was on his home turf in Thuringia. He was able to pick his hiding location well among the caves, bunkers, and mine excavations; the rugged mountainous terrain was ideal for seeking refuge.

A tip to Americans resulted in Sauckel's capture in July 1945, when he was found hiding in a bunker. It seems that the tip came from a "German," but that German was of American birth and citizenship. It was not uncommon for persons of German extraction in far flung parts of the globe to heed the Nazi call and return home to the Fatherland to serve the Nazi regime.

The photo on the next page shows a view looking down the row of bunkers, with Bunker 0 at the left edge of the photo, followed by Workshop 1 (the angled building), then Bunker 1 on the right. Bunker 1 was used for wing assembly. A log house belonging to Gauleiter Fritz Sauckel can be seen in the woods behind and above Workshop 1. *(National Archives, RG 111-SC 203642)*

Bunkers near Weimar

At some point in the summer of 1945 after Sauckel's capture, the American army withdrew, allowing the Soviets to take over the area. It thus became part of the Soviet-dominated German Democratic Republic (a.k.a. East Germany). When the Americans withdrew, they took with them considerable parts of jet engines and rockets, as well as numerous German rocket scientists and engineers. Wernher von Braun was able to recruit a hundred or so of his fellow German rocket scientists to flee from the advancing Soviet Red Army. Wernher von Braun's brother, a Lieutenant in the German Army, commandeered a military truck. Access to the truck permitted von Braun's rocket scientists to flee west and thus evade capture by the Soviets, later surrendering to the Americans. These German rocket scientists and the pieces of aircraft and rockets became instrumental in the American-Soviet postwar space race.

The Nuremburg Trial and Sauckel's Botched Execution

IT'S HARD TO IMAGINE more history being packed into any one weapon, with the possible exception of those used in the Lincoln and Kennedy assassinations, George Custer's personal sidearm, or perhaps General Lee's sword. The summary of the carnage and history of this Sauckel piece defies description.

Let me try to summarize the enormity of the significance of this piece. Its donor was a notorious criminal responsible for 100,000 or more lives lost (recall that Sauckel was the arch-criminal Third Reich's Minister of Labor). Following the unconditional surrender of Germany, Sauckel went into hiding in a cave. He was one of the few Nazis at Nuremberg who remained incensed that he was even placed on trial. At his trial, and even as he said his last words, Sauckel never showed any remorse, only indignation and contempt. In contrast, Albert Speer, Hitler's architect and Sauckel's immediate superior, expressed remorse and received a relatively mild sentence of 20 years' imprisonment. As part of his atonement, Speer went on to write several books spelling out the crimes committed by the Third Reich. When Sauckel learned of his sentence of death by hanging, heard through headphones via an interpreter (as the Nuremberg judgment was spoken in English, not German), Sauckel actually thought (and continued to think up to the moment he was removed from his holding cell for execution) that the English-to-German interpreter had made a mistake. Sauckel's last words were recorded as "Ich sterbe unschuldig, mein Urteil ist ungerecht. Gott beschütze Deutschland!" (*I'm dying innocently, my sentence is not just. God protect Germany!*).

Sauckel's own testimony at the Nuremberg tribunal acknowledged that as many as 5,000,000 forced laborers from the east were brought into Germany under his direction and literally worked to death. Sauckel argued at the court proceedings that such treatment of laborers was an economic wartime necessity and was thus not criminal. Sauckel was found guilty as a war criminal for crimes against humanity and was sentenced to the gallows.

Sauckel (second row, closest to camera) and seven of his co-defendants at the Nuremberg trials [9]. In his hands, Sauckel is holding the headphone set used to listen to the interpreters. Hermann Göring, seated at the far end of the front row, cheated the hangman by ingesting a smuggled cyanide pill just before the scheduled execution.

Deadly Bribe

The Nuremberg hangman in charge of the executions was U.S. Army Master Sergeant John C. Woods, 1903-1950, of San Antonio, Texas. I've read that Woods and his assistant, Joseph Malta, were both Jewish, but I have yet to confirm this. Woods was later quoted in a press interview that he looked forward to the hanging of these Nazis and that he would gladly do it again.

Sauckel and nine other condemned criminals were hanged during the early hours of October 16, 1946. Hermann Göring avoided the hangman by taking a poison pill mere hours beforehand. Sauckel, as well as the other convicted Nazis, was hanged using shorter than customary ropes causing the condemned men to suffer painful strangulation deaths as opposed to quick neck-snapping drops. Sauckel's death by strangulation was so gruesome that it is reported that after the drop on the gallows, Woods and his assistant had to hold onto Sauckel's legs so as to pull him down, thus completing the strangulation. Sauckel was finally pronounced dead after 14 minutes of dangling on the rope.

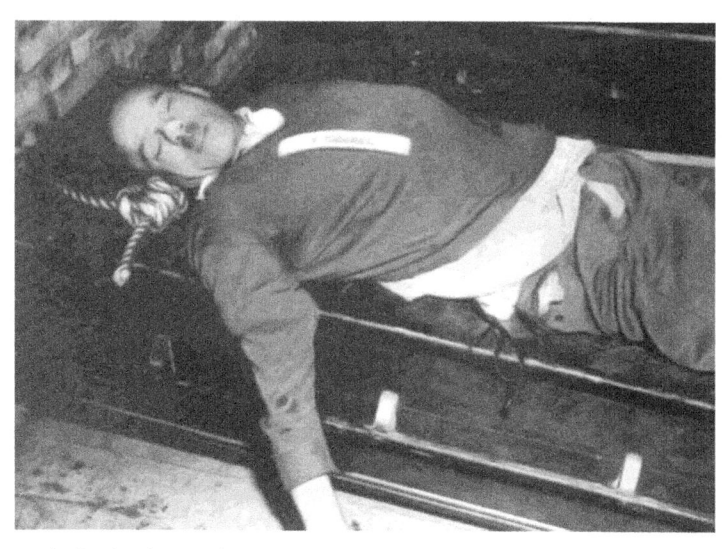

Sauckel's body in the process of assuming ambient temperature following his botched gallows drop, after pronouncement of death, and just prior to his cremation on October 16, 1946

It has been speculated that Woods or possibly his assistant made a calculation error in preparing the ropes. My view, however, is that a professional hangman who hanged some 347 military prisoners over his 15-year military career didn't make a calculation error. He knew his business far too well.

The bodies of the Nuremberg guilty were examined by various international representatives, photographed, and cremated with no fanfare. Within hours, Sauckel's ashes and those of his fellow condemned Nazi war criminals were dumped into an undisclosed ditch somewhere in Germany during a rainy day.

Martin Bormann was tried in absentia, and thus not hanged. Bormann's remains were later identified in the 1970s, but his death was circa 1945.

As an irony, Woods died on July 21, 1950 when he accidently electrocuted himself while working on an electric chair.

Possible Recipients: The Long List

WE HAVE ESTABLISHED with certainty the notorious donor of the presentation pistol, the barbaric organization represented, the notable location of the ceremony, and the historical significance of the event. Now we will turn to the matter of finding the recipient of the Sauckel Walther PP. Short of unearthing photographs or documents that tell of the actual presentation, the research process for identifying the Walther's recipient focuses on making assumptions and then casting a wide net.

I started with the assumption that the recipient's initials were W.B. and generated a list of prominent Nazis with those initials. This list was largely based on the alphabetical listings in the book *Who's Who in Nazi Germany* [1]. I was also aided by several knowledgeable people familiar with Nazi presentation guidelines.

The list below contains seven possible candidates and is presented in alphabetical order.

Werner Best (1903-1989). Werner Best received his doctorate in law (JD) in 1927. He, like many Nazis, was ambitious and worked hard on behalf of the party. Best was instrumental in the plans for Nazi occupation of Western Europe. His plans called for political changes in France, Spain, and even the British Isles. For example, he planned that Spain, after it came under Nazi control, would be divided into three smaller nations.

During the war, he was transferred to Denmark owing to his losing an internal Nazi power struggle. He ruled Denmark as the civilian administrator with some degree of leniency and moderation, as he wanted to create a showcase of how good life could be in an occupied territory. For example, he allowed King Christian X to remain on the throne, along with the Danish parliament as the pseudo governing body. Of the approximately 7,000 Jews in Demark, fewer than ten percent were taken by the Nazis. It was Best's plan to wait to round up the Danish Jews until after the war, so as to create the false wartime impression that Nazis were reasonable masters of countries under their control.

I discount Best as a candidate recipient. I see no motive for Best being honored by Sauckel. Their respective worlds were largely dissimilar. Sauckel's forced workers were of Eastern European origins, not French or Danish.

Werner Best (1903-1989)

Werner von Blomberg (1878-1946). Blomberg was an old school military man. Even though he had risen high in the Nazi hierarchy, he reached his peak circa 1937. By 1938 he had been discharged and largely discredited. He and his younger wife were then forced into exile, with scandal attached, for a year. It is quite unlikely that Sauckel would have accorded the honor of a ceremonial weapon to Blomberg in the late months of 1938.

Walther von Brauchitsch (1881-1948). Brauchitsch was Commander-in-Chief of the German Army from 1938 to 1941. As such, a military type of Brauchitsch's stature would have been honored with a pistol with more emphasis on his rank and position.

Brauchitsch was on the rise in 1938, having been recently appointed Commander-in-Chief in February of that year. Moreover, he was uniformed military. Brauchitsch was a brilliant military strategist and dictated the Nazi *blitzkrieg* or "lightning war" that so devastated and overran much of Eastern Europe in the early years of World War II. Nevertheless, some historians describe Brauchitsch as "meek," as at times he would take abuse and not stand up to attacks, notably from Hitler. Some historians suggest that Brauchitsch was selected for the post to replace General Werner von Fritsch because Brauchitsch was a person who could be manipulated, particularly by Hitler.

The interplay between Hitler and his generals was without question a complex issue and a power struggle. My sense is that Hitler was a common person who came up from the working class. In contrast, the generals tended to be from upper crust classes. The cultural divide was deep. Hitler never trusted his generals. Likewise, the generals distrusted and looked down at Hitler as a lowlife.

During Brauchitsch's tenure as Nazi Commander-in-Chief, as early as late 1939 and into 1940 Hitler made moves to eclipse his generals and personally dictate military plans, methods, and dates. Brauchitsch and his general staff were referred to as the

Oberkommando des Heeres (OKH), which translates to Army High Command. As head of the OKH, Brauchitsch, while brilliantly instrumental in the invasion of Poland, was ultimately blamed and disgraced by Hitler for the failure of the German Armies under his command to take Moscow from the Soviets. He suffered a serious heart attack in late 1941, was dismissed by Hitler, and went into retirement. After Brauchitsch's dismissal on December 19, 1941, Hitler personally took over the duties of Commander-in-Chief.

Brauchitsch with Hitler in Warsaw, October 1939

On May 8, 1945, Brauchitsch was taken prisoner by the Allies. He was subsequently charged with crimes against humanity for having signed (under orders from Hitler) a document at the start of Operation Barbarossa (the invasion of the Soviet Union), the infamous *Kommissarbefehl*, effectively condemning to death all Soviet military and civilians who had been taken prisoner by the invading German forces. Because Brauchitsch was directly tied to such massive atrocities typified by the millions of Soviet, Polish, and Jewish executions as per his orders, his conviction at post-war crime trials was all but certain. Following the war, Brauchitsch was arrested and then incarcerated by the British and held for a time at a camp in Wales. He died in 1948 while awaiting trial as a war criminal after having been transferred back to Hamburg.

Wernher von Braun (1912-1977). Wernher von Braun was the famed German space scientist-engineer who defected to the Allies at the end of the war. Von Braun has to be considered as he was stationed in or near Weimar, where the Germans concentrated their research on rockets and jet engines. The likelihood of Wernher von Braun as a candidate recipient, however, is small based on his young age (26 at the time) and the attitude that scientists like von Braun, while helpful to the Third Reich, were used and otherwise taken for granted. In general, they were not given public recognition in the form of an inscribed presentation pistol.

Wilhelm von Brückner (1884-1954). From the early start of the Nazi party in the 1920s, Brückner served for a long period as Hitler's close confidant, adjutant, crony, and personal bodyguard. In late 1940, however, Hitler sacked Brückner, who was then assigned to other duties for the balance of the war. Nonetheless, in November of 1938 Brückner was integral to Hitler's inner circle.

Brückner, along with Adolf Hitler and Fritz Sauckel, was instrumental in the 1923 attempted Weimar Republic overthrow (which involved a total of about 20 insider conspirators), known as the Munich Beer Hall Putsch. The Beer Hall Putsch ended in violence and open gunfire between the Nazi party instigators and the police in Munich. Sixteen Nazis were killed, but most of them were lesser known supporters. In the return fire, four Munich police were killed. Additional people were injured, such as Hermann Göring who received two bullet wounds. Göring was still able to flee to Austria and escape arrest.

The conspirators were sentenced to prison for varying terms as a result. An amnesty permitted the instigators to be released early. Brückner received a sentence of one-and-a-half years, but was released after serving four months. Hitler received a five-year sentence and was incarcerated in the Landsberg Prison in Bavaria. Hitler was released in 1924 after serving less than one year. Although confined, his incarceration did not involve hard labor. While imprisoned, Hitler was free to receive visitors and was able to spend his time writing. It was during this prison time that Hitler wrote his famous *Mein Kampf,* dictating it to his deputy Rudolf Hess, also imprisoned. It was also at this time that Hitler and his inner gang recognized that they had to adopt legal means to bring down the Weimar Republic's government, which they finally accomplished in 1933.

Wilhelm von Brückner (1884-1954)

Pertaining to the photograph above of Brückner, his two lapel bars are that of an Oberführer, equivalent to a Brigadier General. The matter of rank is somewhat confusing. Some authorities call this Senior Colonel, whereas others translate it as Brigadier. Brückner was later promoted to SS Lieutenant-General (SS-Obergruppenführer). The abbreviation "SS" stands for Schutzstaffel, which means "protective guard." The SS was originally a group of 280 who protected Hitler in the early 1920s, but it grew to about 250,000 members under the command of Himmler. The SS ran the concentration camps and operated the Holocaust. Fritz Sauckel, Walter Buch, Werner Best, and Wilhelm von Brückner all held honorary ranks in the SS.

This earlier signed photo of Brückner shows him with the rank of Oberführer. The white military uniform was quite rare.

For somewhat complex reasons Brückner had a falling out with Hitler on October 18, 1940, and as a result was transferred to other duties, out of the sphere of Hitler's inner circle. The details of Hitler sacking Brückner were related to an underling Hitler had dismissed. Brückner is said to have intervened to assert that the underling was blameless. Hitler in his rage turned on Brückner saying, in effect, "Well, you're fired too!"

Hitler was prone to outbursts, as well as believing in horoscopes and other illogical dark arts. One such superstitious art was to pour molten lead into punch vessels, usually on New Year's Eve. Hitler used the shapes formed from the lead as it solidified in a chaotic manner to make predictions of the future. Rational thinking was not Hitler's strong suit.

Some sources suggest that Brückner was hung out to dry, as others coveted being close to Hitler and thus plotted against the affable Brückner, notably Martin Bormann.

My sense is that this falling out worked in Brückner's favor, as he was removed from Hitler's immediate circle and was not with Hitler in the Berlin bunker as the Red Army closed in, in April 1945. Brückner was captured by U.S. forces. Also, Brückner was able to be viewed (from a post-war perspective) as a military officer as opposed to a war criminal by the time of the Nuremberg trials. At Nuremburg, Brückner did provide testimony, but he himself was not on trial before that international court.

Internet documents show that Brückner was interrogated by the Western Allies, first on June 22, 1945 (at the Seventh Army Interrogation Center, interrogation number SAIC/PIR/3), and again on October 31, 1945 (by Operational Intelligence, interrogation number OI/PIR/24). An Internet reference to the book *Secrets of the SS*, by Glenn B. Infield [11], states that Brückner was placed on trial for his Nazi-related activities. Brückner was tried not by the Allies but rather by the post-war German authorities as part of a denazification program, which was initiated on June 1, 1946. The German judges were more lenient than the Allied judges. As a result, Brückner was sentenced to three years. Brückner lived past the war, dying in Bavaria at the age of 69 on August 18, 1954.

Walter Buch (1883-1949) was President of the Nazi Party's Supreme Court. Buch still remains a rather mysterious person from the standpoint of history. Justice Walter Buch was strongly anti-Semitic and powerful within the Third Reich. As a judge he used his power to settle disputes within the party. Hitler was the only one above Buch with the power to reverse Buch's rulings. Buch in his rulings allowed the events of the Kristallnacht (November 9, 1938) to go largely unpunished, effectively legalizing Nazi party brutality, and even placed the guilt on the Jews.

I find the closeness of the presentation date, a mere four days prior to Kristallnacht, to be significant. I conclude that Walter Buch stands out as a strong candidate as the recipient of the subject Sauckel Model PP Walther pistol. Sauckel in late 1938 wanted two things: factories previously under Jewish ownership and forced laborers. The ruling by Buch blaming the Jews caused the Jews to lose both citizenship and property rights, thus granting Sauckel both of his wishes.

After the war, Buch was seized by U.S. troops, tried, and sentenced to five years in prison. In 1949 he committed suicide by slitting his wrists and then throwing himself into the Ammersee (a lake in Upper Bavaria). Buch held the honorary rank of *SS Gruppenführer*, given to him in 1934.

Walther Buhle (1894-1959) was an infantry general, whereupon he was promoted to Chief of the Army Staff (of the OKH) in 1942. Buhle was present in the bunker in East Prussia on July 20, 1944 when the assassination attempt on Hitler took place. Later in the war he was placed in charge of armament factories. Buhle's interest and understanding of factory arms production serves as justification for Buhle to move onto the short list of candidate recipients.

Following the war, Buhle was detained by the Allies and transported to America where he assisted the Allies in sorting through massive quantities of captured Nazi documents and records.

In listing these candidates above, all with the initials W.B., one striking coincidence is that all survived the war, all were taken into custody by Western Allies (thus excluding those captured by Soviets), all were tried and served time in prison, and all, with the exception of Walter Buch, died of natural causes.

Military or Civilian?

AS GERMANY GROUND DOWN INTO DEFEAT in April and May of 1945, people within the Nazi party and its power structure were running for cover. It is not logical to me that a civilian managerial type would have been subjected to the ritual of a formal surrender and in the process being required to surrender his sidearm. In contrast, uniformed ranking officers were obligated to formally surrender, and at that time give up their arms as a part of the ritual. Lower-ranking officers and enlisted men were instructed to dispose of their weapons into piles as they were processed by the Allies, with rifle bolts and munitions placed into separate piles.

My reasoning suggests that a managerial or political civilian type would be apt to take the path of least resistance and discreetly dispose of any firearm in his possession by dropping it into a river or well, or burying it in a shallow hole. A firearm with the type of inscription found on the subject pistol was close to an arrest warrant and war-crimes trial, as it indicated that the person possessing it was a ranking Nazi. Given the choice, a low-key inconspicuous disposal would have happened long before any confrontation with the occupation forces of the Allies.

Of course, the assumption that the firearm was handed over at the time of the recipient's surrender has potential flaws. As a fact of war, people at times get shot and their sidearms are removed from their lifeless bodies. Another possibility is that the subject firearm was inside a house or building and merely taken by a soldier conducting a search. The possibilities are many.

When Germany surrendered in May of 1945, the act of surrender meant that all German civil law and military law ceased. The authority fell into the hands of the victors, in this case the coalition of Allies. As a result, in an effort to avoid arrest and possible trial, it was commonplace for Germans—civilians and military alike—to attempt to blend into the background to appear as innocent as possible. It was also commonplace for the Germans to destroy or hide any incriminating evidence that might be used against them in later trials. The tasks of the occupation armies were to restore order, seize arms and contraband, and screen the German population to ferret out possible culprits. Prominent Nazi party members were high on the suspect list, along with all higher-ranking military officers, especially officers with SS connections.

Had I been in the shoes of a prominent political leader I would have made every effort to destroy or hide any evidence of my connections to the Nazi organization. If I had been the civilian or political recipient, say, of an engraved presentation Walther Model PP similar to the subject piece, my first move would have been to use a simple screwdriver to remove the grips that had my initials inscribed thereon. I would then smash the inscribed grips beyond recognition and throw them into a well or sewer drain. I would toss the firearm itself in pieces into the nearest river. If no river was handy, the next best choice would have been to bury the remain in a shallow hole—and the quicker the better. Recall that in 1945, modern-day metal detectors were not yet available. Burying was, at that time, a fairly safe method of disposal.

Yet another motivation for Germans to ditch their firearms stemmed from the terms of the surrender of Germany. The Allies had enacted martial law, and one facet was that Germans were no longer allowed to legally possess firearms. All firearms had to be turned over to the occupying Allies. Accordingly, firearms had zero value, and at times negative value, to a German. Any German discovered still possessing a firearm risked severe penalties. In most cases there was little room for negotiation. Punishment, if one was caught, was harsh and swift. The priority of virtually all Germans at this point was to remain alive and survive from day to day. Firearms would be tossed away, securely hidden, or turned in, provided the surrender of the firearm didn't bring unnecessary attention.

In the early days of my research, I ventured a guess that a uniformed military man might be the recipient of the pistol. One of my sources, an avid collector and Sauckel expert, respectfully makes clear (below) that he questions my supposition, and as such I have now amended my thinking to agree with him. He writes:

"Identifying other participants in the (Weimar) event that had similar initials will be a daunting task. I have a re-print of a listing of political leaders in Gau Thüringen that was originally published in the late 1930s. If the initials are W.B., I found at least two very senior political leaders with those initials who would have been at the Gau event. But like I wrote, I think the inclusion of the name of the Stiftung indicates that this pistol was a presentation to someone who was there concerning the management of the Stiftung who Sauckel would have wanted to honor. If it was intended to be a presentation of a political nature, I think the inscription would have reflected that intent. Of course, that is just my opinion."

A factor in the search for the recipient is that other Sauckel presentation pieces exist. As time passes and more research continues, it should be possible to observe trends as to the types of persons honored as recipients. Based on this, it stands to reason that we should be able to substantiate my source's viewpoint, or the converse.

I agree completely that the net of possibilities should initially be cast as wide as feasible. However, the search process becomes simplified whenever any ineligible candidate is eliminated. My logic and training as a mathematician lead me to simplify any problem whenever possible. My intuition leans toward a uniformed recipient and/or ranking party official and thus a tighter net as contrasted to my source's suggestion

To summarize my expert source's assertion:

"I think the inclusion of the name of the Stiftung indicates that this pistol was a presentation to someone who was there concerning the management of the Stiftung who Sauckel would have wanted to honor."

My assessment is that if indeed the recipient was a managerial type or even some non-uniformed civilian politician, the odds go way against the specimen Walther PP ending up in the hands of an American soldier. First, the civilian would not have had much motivation to surrender, much less with a firearm. Second, the surrender or discovery would have been most likely delayed as it took time (in some extreme cases years and even decades) for the Allies to screen the German populace in search of wanted Nazi criminals as well as contraband. Thuringia was held for only a brief period by the American and British forces. Within several months (by mid-summer of 1945) after Germany's surrender, the Thuringia portion of Germany was handed over to the Soviets and thus became known as East Germany during the post-war era.

As I reexamine my source's statement above, let me offer my way of restating his point. The point he's making is that if the honor was to be bestowed upon someone of Brauchitsch's ranking (and external to the inner workings of the Wilhelm Gustloff Stiftung Association), then his name would have been inscribed on the piece. Because the name of the Wilhelm Gustloff Stiftung is inscribed, this infers that the person honored was somehow connected to the Wilhelm Gustloff Stiftung, such as in a managerial position. At the risk of splitting hairs and thus looking stupid, I wish to explain why I consider the recipient being internal as unlikely. The inscription starts (in German) with von der… I translate such usage as "from the" or possibly "of the." In English one might say "Given on behalf of…". I suggest that the phrasing implies a gift from the Wilhelm Gustloff organization and thus given to a recipient outside of its structure. I see the presentation as having been given to a deserving recipient not affiliated with the organization. Therefore, I conclude that Sauckel didn't give this to a person already under his authority, but rather someone who Sauckel wanted some control over—to be able to seek a future favor from.

Of course, this remains as an open topic. I am not in a position to entirely discount or underestimate my source's views. One factor does bother me, however, and that concerns the inclusion of the date, which ties the presentation piece to the Thuringia Gautag itself. My thinking is that if an honored guest was to arrive, a tour of the factory might have been appropriate. In my professional life I have seen that at the conclusion of a tour, the tour host then honors the distinguished guest with a token of appreciation and to commemorate the event. In those cases, the date as well as the credit to the donor would have been included on the inscription.

The fact that some American officer or enlisted GI ended up with the subject Model PP strongly suggests that it was a sidearm of a prominent officer in uniform or ranking Nazi official, and that person was either captured or was obligated to formally surrender, giving up his sidearm as a part of the surrender ritual. This line of reasoning forces me to return to uniformed ranking officers and party officials. At that point the candidate list gets to be short indeed. Walther von Brauchitsch, Wilhelm von Brückner, Walter Buch, Werner Best, and Walther Buhle satisfy all conditions: they were senior enough to have deserved the presentation pistol, they each were uniformed or were ranking party officials, and were identifiable at the time of Germany's surrender. In addition, all five of these candidates were taken into custody by Allied military. Hiding their identity to the Allies and trying to blend into the masses as an obscure private or corporal would not have been options for Brauchitsch, Brückner, Buch, Best, and Buhle. All five were well known to the Allies by photographs and other captured and/or public documents.

One possible way to fast track the unraveling of the mystery would be to ascertain which army performed the actual capture of each man. Because the subject Walther Model PP ended up in the hands of an American, it stands to reason that the Americans (rather than the British, the French, or the Soviets) initially took the recipient into custody. It is known that Braun, Brückner, and Buch were taken into custody by Americans.

My logic expressed above in these few paragraphs does not finalize the recipient issue, but it does allow me to follow a line of plausible reasoning and to be comfortable enough to move on. Until such time that other evidence surfaces to contradict my assumption, I am content to operate under the hypothesis that the recipient was within this short list of candidates: General Walther von Brauchitsch, Nazi Supreme Court Judge Walter Buch, and lastly General Walther Buhle.

It remains a challenging and daunting task to identify the actual recipient beyond the circumstantial evidence, but I remain hopeful that positive identification will be established at some point. Moreover, other names still need to be considered as they might be identified.

Narrowing the Search: The Short List

FROM THE "LONG LIST" of seven potential candidate recipients, all prominent Nazis with the initials W.B., I used my below assumptions to develop a shorter list with only three names. My final step was to consider the merits and thus likelihood of each of the respective shortlisted three.

The first assumption (which was strongly advised by my expert source mentioned in the previous chapter) was that this particular presentation Model PP was given to a civilian as opposed to a ranking military type.

A second assumption was that the Walther Model PP was given to a person of stature external to Sauckel's organization. I have already reasoned that Sauckel wanted a favor. Those within Sauckel's authority would follow his orders, whereas bribes were commonplace in getting cooperation from outside parties, particularly a bribe in the form of a coveted engraved pistol.

A third assumption was that the recipient at some point became well enough known by the Allies to be targeted for surrender, interrogation, and possible trial.

My last assumption was that the recipient surrendered to Americans, and not British, French, or Soviets. As an aside, German military taken by the Soviets tended to cease to exist. The

Germans in their advance into Russia had killed millions. When the tide of war turned against Germany, the Soviets returned the favor in kind.

As I use my imagination to reconstruct events at the Weimar Gautag, I envision a giant and gala gathering. Nothing was last-minute. There were few sideshows. As such, the presentation of the Sauckel Walther was incorporated into the main agenda. I therefore discount the idea that the pistol was presented during some minor event, like a factory tour.

Hitler and other dignitaries were in attendance at the 1938 Weimar Gautag. As host of the large and festive Gautag, Sauckel's attention would have been exclusively focused on the center of power and ambitious plans for Nazi expansion and world dominance. Sauckel wouldn't involve himself in a small side tour. The presentation was definitely a scheduled event. The recipient was a high-level Nazi. This reasoning supports a short list of candidate recipients. This list, in order of least likely to most likely, is: Brauchitsch, Buhle, and Buch.

As a scientist, I have come to rely heavily on forming a working hypothesis and taking a plunge. With this disclaimer in mind, I conjecture that the recipient was from my stated short list of Brauchitsch, Buhle, and Buch. Of these three candidates, I lean towards Buch. He was the only civilian on my short list.

Kristallnacht, the "Night of Broken Glass," was only four days into the future. History records that an assassination occurred on Monday, November 7, 1938. A Jewish 17-year-old who had been living in France for several years learned that the Nazis had exiled his parents to Poland from Hanover, Germany, where they had lived for years. As retaliation, the enraged teenager shot Ernst vom Rath, a prominent Nazi in Paris.

Joseph Goebbels, Hitler's Chief of Propaganda, had been planning to take action against German Jews. The assassination provided him with the excuse he needed to launch a pogrom against the Jews. He seized the opportunity to rile Hitler's supporters into an anti-Semitic frenzy.

On the night of November 9/10, 1938, Nazis in Germany torched synagogues, vandalized Jewish homes, schools, and businesses, and killed close to 100 Jews. In the aftermath of Kristallnacht, some 30,000 Jewish men were arrested and sent to Nazi concentration camps. Over 100,000 Jews fled Germany for other countries after Kristallnacht, which had obviously been well-organized and planned in advance.

The Nazis suffered no serious consequences internationally, leading them to believe they could get away with the mass murder that was the Holocaust, in which an estimated six million European Jews died.

Plans for Kristallnacht were in place before the weekend of the Gautag; the tinder box was already staged and Goebbels was just waiting for the spark. Sauckel was obviously privy to these plans and would have provided Buch with a bribe—an incentive—for a favorable court ruling. Supreme Court Justice Walter Buch in turn gave Sauckel what he wanted: a ruling that the Jews were to blame for Kristallnacht. This ruling resulted in Jews in Germany and occupied territories losing property rights and citizenship.

Again, I conjecture: the recipient of the Walther PP presentation pistol was Supreme Court Justice Walter Buch. Although photographs show Buch in SS uniform, he was a civilian. His rank in the SS was honorary. Buch was in the unique position to give Sauckel a favor: the ruling that in turn stripped the Jews in Germany of both citizenship and property. No other candidate with initials W.B. can come close.

Because my conjecture has not been supported by hard evidence, two Nazi generals, Buhle and Brauchitsch, must also be considered. Buhle had strong connections to factories and arms production. Brauchitsch must also remain in consideration as then Nazi Commander-in-Chief.

With my working Buch hypothesis stated, I will now delve deeper into all three short-listed candidates, in order from least likely to most likely.

Walther von Brauchitsch. General Brauchitsch was the fifth son of a Prussian German cavalry general. His service in the German military spanned over four decades, from 1900 to 1941. In 1938 he was appointed Commander-in-Chief of the German Army. He oversaw the very successful invasion of Poland. It was Brauchitsch who initially laid out the plans to invade France by way of the low countries. Brauchitsch's plan, given the code name "Case Yellow," followed closely the German invasion of France in 1914. One Internet source comments that a critical security breach occurred on January 10, 1940, when a German aircraft carrying the Case Yellow plans and several knowledgeable persons strayed in bad weather and was forced down in an area to the west controlled by the Allies.

Other generals, notably General Erich von Manstein (1887-1973), had even in 1939 argued for changes to the Case Yellow plan, considering it to be flawed and lacking the essence of total victory. Because of a number of factors and after much intrigue, Hitler ordered on February 17, 1940 that Manstein's plan for the invasion of France be adopted instead. As such, history associates General Erich von Manstein as being the author and mastermind of the invasion of France, but bear in mind that Brauchitsch was still the Commander-in-Chief of the German war machine at that time and the primary author of the original Case Yellow plan. There is little question that Manstein's plan worked with enormous benefit to the Nazis. It used deception as well as concentrated strength of armored units to trick and then ensnare the French, British, and Belgian armies in a massive trap that resulted in Dunkirk.

In the period from the fall of 1939 until late in 1941, Brauchitsch remained as Commander-in-Chief. However, he was more and more subject to following Hitler's directives and war plans. Brauchitsch's ultimate fall from grace came about because of the failure of the German Armies to take Moscow during the campaign in Russia in late 1941. Brauchitsch had argued (directly to Hitler) against Hitler's invasion plans for the attack on Russia (Operation Barbarossa), feeling that the plan was flawed and contrary to proper military strategy. Brauchitsch advised that in the fall of 1941 the advancing German armies should solidify their positions and wait until spring of 1942, whereas Hitler wanted it all—and now. Hitler ordered that the multiple attacks on Moscow, Stalingrad, and the Caucasus be advanced simultaneously, despite the approach of the Russian winter.

Walther von Brauchitsch (1881-1948)

As I read various accounts of the events of WWII, my sense is that Brauchitsch was incredibly disciplined as a traditional Prussian military soldier carrying out war according to rules, and even let me say, chivalry. In contrast, Hitler was vastly more unscrupulous, cunning, and ruthless, as well as obsessed with power. Even as early as the period following the collapse of Poland in late 1939, Brauchitsch had offered his resignation to Hitler, but Hitler refused to accept it. It would appear that Brauchitsch's approach to military affairs presumed that facts and logic mattered and thus would prevail, and that using diplomatic negotiations could help prevent many confrontations from turning to actual outbreak. Hitler and Churchill both remained resolute in their respective positions, not an inch was ceded, and so hostilities ensued. There was to be no negotiated peace. Hitler's genius at power-broking and hence his early successes elevated his ego, which in the end caused his downfall.

Historically speaking of the events in Russia, I am reminded of General James Longstreet's similar attempts to convince General Robert E. Lee that a frontal charge at Gettysburg in 1863 was preordained to fail. In Longstreet's case, however, Lee was man enough to later accept the blame as being his alone. In contrast Brauchitsch, even though he had voiced strong opposition to Hitler's plans, even directly to Hitler, was severely chastised and demeaned by Hitler for the defeat.

Brauchitsch suffered a serious heart attack and withdrew from service in December 1941. According to one Internet source, he retired to his home in Schleswig-Holstein (the area just south of Denmark). A second Internet source disputes this, claiming that Brauchitsch spent the retirement war years in a hunting lodge near Prague.

As previously stated, on May 8, 1945, Brauchitsch was taken prisoner by Allied forces and was charged with crimes against humanity.

It is not well known, but Brauchitsch opposed many of Hitler's war plans. He went along nonetheless rather than make waves. He also was sympathetic to the German generals under his command in 1938 who plotted to overthrow Hitler, but he remained a neutral bystander rather than lend any support.

Brauchitsch's stature as recently promoted Commander-in-Chief of the German Army in February 1938 makes him, in my view, a possible candidate recipient of the subject Walther PP. Until such time that hard evidence surfaces to positively name the recipient, Brauchitsch must remain a contender. His rank and stature were formidable. On the less likely side, however, military generals like Brauchitsch were usually honored with engraved pistols suggesting such stature, and this pistol does not specify any specific military rank.

Walther von Brauchitsch on the cover of Time magazine

During the early phases of WWII, Brauchitsch was even well known and acknowledged in the west, as his photograph made the covers of popular American magazines, notably *Time* and

Newsweek. *Life* magazine covered him as well. Charismatic is yet another adjective that historians associate with Walther von Brauchitsch. Brauchitsch is regarded as one of the more capable of all WWII-era Nazi generals, although many historians regard Field Marshal Erich von Manstein as being the overall best.

Despite his infectious smile, Brauchitsch was far from being your kind and charming next-door neighbor. As Hitler was preparing for the invasion of England, known as Operation Sea Lion, Brauchitsch as Commander-in-Chief had already directed that after the successful conquest of Britain all able-bodied males in England between specific ages (teens and up through age 37) would be rounded up and deported to Europe for purposes of slave labor. In addition, Brauchitsch's plans included provisions that the resources and assets in England would be confiscated and taken back to the continent under German control. These measures would have made the events of German atrocities in Poland mild in comparison. In Poland, the executions and cruelty were aimed at segments of certain Poles, intellectuals, and targeted minorities considered to be inferior, whereas Brauchitsch's plan for occupation of Britain would have been much more universal and by far harsher.

Brauchitsch died in 1948, less than a month after his 67th birthday, while awaiting trial for his crimes.

Walther Buhle. Buhle remains as yet another plausible candidate recipient. My research to date on Buhle is scanty, however he, like so many of the other candidates, had a long and deep association with the Third Reich. Upon his capture at the end of the war, he was considered one of the highest-ranking surviving Nazi generals as he was taken to the United States to assist with the documentation of mountains of captured Third Reich documents. That stemmed from his having been Chief of Staff of the OKH during the closing years of the war. During the timeframe of the presentation, November 1938, Buhle was an infantry general but nonetheless high placed.

Walther Buhle [12]

I have enjoyed reading the book *The German Generals Talk* by noted British military historian B. H. Liddell Hart [13]. Hart interviewed many of the surviving German generals, and thus paints a detailed picture of their inner workings as they conducted the war and interacted with Hitler. Hart notes that at various stages of the war, Hitler would contact Buhle to obtain up-to-date production numbers and such. This stemmed from Buhle being in charge of armament factories. Yes, Fritz Sauckel was the head of the Wilhelm Gustloff Stiftung, but his focus was narrower, devoted mostly to small arms and weapons. In contrast, Buhle oversaw Germany's factories in general, which produced everything from locomotives to tanks to shovels. My speculation is that Buhle didn't become a factories expert overnight, so we must ponder what role he would have played at the time of the Thuringia Gautag in November 1938.

Walter Buch. Historically speaking, Walter Buch remains a relatively unknown person within the Third Reich, but his name certainly has to be held in consideration. His Nazi roots extended deep, as he was active in the formation of the Nazi party in the early 1920s. He had close associations to Hitler, Göring, and others. While not directly involved in the Munich Beer Hall Putsch of 1923, he was sufficiently involved at that time with the party that he sought refuge outside of Germany. Göring called for Buch's return to Germany shortly following the Putsch. Martin Bormann married Buch's daughter Gerda in 1929, with Hitler present at the wedding.

Walter Buch (1883-1949)

In 1934, Hitler ordered a "Blood Purge" of the Nazis, assassinating anyone whom he believed could become a political enemy in the future. Buch took sadistic enjoyment in watching his victims die, some of them old Party comrades whom he killed with his own hand. During the Third Reich, no one was safe from the hatred or vengeance of the supreme executioner of the Party.

Buch was not only cruel, but also strongly anti-Semitic, and did not hesitate to claim that Jews were outside the law. On October 21, 1938, Buch wrote: "The Jew is not a human being. He is an appearance of putrescence."

As the Nazi party came to power, its acquisition of that power depended on key legal rulings—which Buch provided. Buch presided over the Nazi Party Supreme Court's secret investigation into Kristallnacht and ruled that the Nazis who had murdered close to a hundred Jews were innocent of any crime and were only obeying orders.

After the war, Buch was taken into custody by U.S. forces in Munich.

Of the short list three, Buch by far was in the best position to provide a significant favor to Sauckel. By any measure, as Nazi Supreme Court Justice, Walter Buch could give Sauckel what Sauckel desperately needed: formerly Jewish-owned factories and access to forced laborers. The court ruling by Walter Buch greased the rails for the Nazis to strip the Jews of their citizenship and properties. Therefore, I stand on my hypothesis that the recipient was Justice Walter Buch. This hypothesis is also supported by the incredible closeness in timing of the Weimar Gautag and the events of Kristallnacht. The widespread destruction throughout Germany and occupied Austria aimed at Jews was planned and in place at the Weimar Gautag.

Given the plausibility of Buch being the recipient, I'd like to speculate on the identity of the U.S. officer or enlisted man who brought the Model PP presentation pistol back to America.

As the war's end came, large-scale resistance ended. Some diehard pockets remained, but the conquering Allied forces made large advances, often by driving into cities where all opposition had ceased. Considerable numbers of German military units and individuals were waving the white flag and surrendering. German military was eager to seek out American forces rather than be taken by the Soviets.

Walter Buch was a civilian, but as a high-ranking known Nazi, he was also sought. Buch was then in Munich, Germany. Munich was taken on April 30, 1945 and occupied by four U.S. divisions: the U.S. 3rd, 42nd, and 45th Infantry Divisions and the 20th Armored Division. Two divisions were from Patton's 3rd Army, with the other two divisions being from the 7th Army. Patton's diary establishes that Patton was in Nuremberg at that time. The three infantry divisions, being more likely to take prisoners, were commanded as follows: Commanding officer of the U.S. 3rd Infantry Division was Major General John W. O'Daniel, nicknamed Iron Mike. O'Daniel was known for collecting war trophies. One of O'Daniel's proudest trophies from World War II was a pair of Hermann Göring's large trousers. He called them "a lot of pants." After the war, O'Daniel lived in Georgia, Virginia, and Hawaii in the early 1950s.

The commanding officer of the 42nd was Major General Harry J. Collins. Collins was a native of Chicago, Illinois, but was stationed at Camp Atterbury, Indiana in the early 1950s, where he commanded the 31st Infantry Division until retiring from the army in 1954.

Major General Robert T. Frederick was the commanding officer of the 45th Infantry Division. Frederick was promoted to the two-star rank of major general at the young age of 37 and given command of the 45th Infantry Division on December 3, 1944. He retired on disability in March 1952.

It's possible that Buch surrendered to one of the three or to one of their senior officers. I have been unable to conclusively determine if any of them has a direct connection to the Akron, Ohio area, where my father purchased the subject Walther during a work trip to a factory.

My instincts suggest that any officer of two-star stature would not have been later employed doing factory work. Moreover, a two-star general would have never sold such a war trophy for a mere $75. The person who sold it to my father was possibly lower on the food chain—thus willing to hand it over on a whim for some green money. Perhaps the pistol subsequently found its way into the hands of a family member or friend who then tired of it, or had plenty of other pistols. As a kid I can recall displays of war trophies such as swords, Nazi youth organization knives, helmets, and the like. In that era, war trophies were relatively commonplace. A collector with excess would commonly give a trophy to a younger brother or neighbor. Whoever sold it to my father didn't value the piece and wasn't tied to it emotionally. The unknown seller in Ohio sold it to my father for a quick buck.

Another possibility, although remote, is that the seller was impressed with my father as a man. Pop was a soldier working on the home front. The Model PP could have been a tribute to my father. Who knows?

Yet another possibility is that an enlisted man or a lower-ranking officer from one of the Infantry Divisions occupying Munich somehow got hold of the pistol and managed to smuggle it home, only to sell it eight years later. Troops occupying a city like Munich would establish checkpoints at critical intersections and bridges. Homes would be searched with troops going door to door. Because Walter Buch was a civilian and not uniformed, it was likely he was at his home. Records show that Buch was taken by U.S. forces on April 30, on the first day of occupation. That would have been a tumultuous day filled with many actions, seizures, and surrenders. Buch's surrender was likely to have been a routine occurrence when viewed in perspective.

I can say one thing with certainty: My father laid the Model PP on the kitchen table in 1953 upon his return from a job assignment in Eastern Ohio. While I can't say for certain the exact journey this firearm took from Germany to our family's kitchen, my best guess is that it was at one time owned by Walter Buch.

Photographic Records

Hitler's general staff, June 1940 [8]

THE ABOVE PHOTOGRAPH is of Hitler's general staff, also known as the field staff, circa June 1940. Hitler is at center. Most of the garments appear to have been slept in, as they look not freshly pressed, along with dirty boots, thus suggesting travel.

Obviously, experts have the ability to name all those photographed, but I will do only a partial identification. Wilhelm

Brückner, Hitler's adjutant, is the tall man to the far left, front row. Of note also is Heinrich Hoffmann (1885-1957), the shorter man front row, extreme right (with hand on hip). Hoffmann was famed as the official photographer of Hitler.

The Hoffmann photographic record of the Third Reich has been declared by the Allied Forces as public domain, so copyrights are usually not an issue. This photograph would appear to have been taken in a secure location, since we see no evidence of bodyguard posturing. My speculation is that Hoffmann had set up the camera on a tripod, and then stepped in at the last moment so as to be included.

Hoffmann's role is still being played out in the saga related to the subject Walther PP, as Hoffmann took tens upon tens of thousands of photographs over his career. These are now archived in a large library collection in Munich and are still being studied by World War II scholars. I hope that at some point in the future, photographic evidence will definitively prove the identity of the pistol's recipient.

Obviously, without proof such as a photograph of the presentation or other documentation, the recipient's identity won't be an absolute certainty. But because the Third Reich photographs still exist, in the tens of thousands, I am ever hopeful that a day will come when the recipient will be positively identified.

Wartime Diaries and Private Documents

THE PERSONAL LETTERS, DIARIES, AND JOURNALS of many prominent Nazis such as von Brückner and von Brauchitsch were spoils of war and have largely vanished. Yet other documents have been preserved, now often in the form of microfilm images, and await the tedious process of being researched, catalogued, and ultimately made accessible electronically. This is a slow and arduous endeavor.

It's plausible that some soldier took such journals as war booty, and these have never surfaced. Yet other diaries of high-ranking Nazis were deliberately destroyed in order to cover up any incriminating evidence that could be used in a war trials court against them. Bombings and the perils of war obliterated still more. While it must be assumed that many wartime diaries were lost forever, many other documents exist, which help us piece together a partial story. As more and more archives are converted into electronic format and put online, much research can be conducted using the Internet, which is both inexpensive and doesn't require travel. The Internet search engines continue to reveal new and useful information at virtually every click of the mouse.

Getting War Booty Home

WE CAN ASSUME that the American who liberated the piece and brought it back home was exercising the "finders keepers" practice. It may have been the officer to whom the recipient surrendered. Or maybe the returning soldier just picked it up or won it in a craps game on ship. Those details will most likely never be known.

Few today realize that getting booty from WWII back home from the European theatre was both perilous and nontrivial. In the field it was reported that some commanding Allied Generals, one being General Mark Clark in Italy, confiscated trophy pieces from rank-and-file troops. As such, combat and line soldiers were reluctant to adhere to rules and procedures requiring disclosure and documentation.

Returning GIs boarded transport ships where each soldier was limited to what he could carry crammed into his single duffle bag. Duffle bags were subject to searches, so as to keep grenades, live ammo, and even landmines from endangering voyages. Once on a crowded troop ship, there was little private space, and less opportunity to protect one's goods or stash from theft. Troop ships were so crowded that the concept of "hot beds" at times governed. Each bed was used by three GIs wherein each would have his eight hours of sleep, only to be ousted in turn and another GI would get into the "hot bed" for the next eight hours. Also, sleeping on an open deck in the elements was not uncommon.

I recall my uncles telling me stories from WWII about how one could guard their stashed goods almost 24 hours daily, but going to the head or the mess was when goods stashed inside duffle bags (left unguarded next to a bunk or hammock) were stolen. Another hazard was the shakedown. Officers in charge of ships using the equivalent of military police detachments would conduct unannounced shakedowns, bow to stern, looking in every bag and nook and cranny in search of contraband. GIs who were being shaken down, or sensing a pending shakedown, would often opt to throw booty out a porthole as opposed to getting caught with contraband. Getting back home after years at war was the first priority. Getting war booty home was quite secondary. According to the stories I heard as a kid, significant quantities of captured booty and war trophies were pitched out of portholes on the voyages home.

As kids, my brothers and I were spellbound as we listened to the stories of combat, army life, boredom, and even getting war booty home. The stories were told by various uncles, friends of family, friends from church, and also by the male teachers in school who had returned from overseas. My seventh-grade social studies teacher was Ernest Schultz, who served in the airborne in Europe. My high school mathematics teacher was a strange man, Mr. Robert Harrison, who served as support staff for bomber crews flying out of England. When a class got to be boring, or if time needed to be filled, these teachers would tell story after story of war events and action. My uncle Eddie was an infantry combat soldier in France and later Germany. Eddie was one who brought home considerable war stash and booty. Eddie also complained that much of his really good stuff had been stolen from him while on the ship coming back home.

As a somewhat worldly (and thus less naïve) person, it has

become clear to me that a supporting motivation for the shakedown was often the greed of the officers in charge on the ship, who could benefit by confiscating discovered goods for their own personal gain. This would be akin to present day police who secret away fine firearms from evidence rooms as well as firearms voluntarily surrendered to police by gullible members of the public. Obviously, returning military officers had the luxury of more lax rules (compared to enlisted men) on the return of war booty.

Family Provenance of the Pistol

ONE OF THE MOST FREQUENT QUESTIONS I am asked is, "How did you come into possession of this Sauckel Walther PP?" Let me explain.

My father (Albert W. Kraus, 1910-1993) acquired the Sauckel piece in 1953. At that time he brought it home to Fairfield, Connecticut following a Bullard's "job" in the Akron, Ohio area. Pop was a traveling machinist or field service representative who serviced large industrial machines for Bullard Machine Tool Company of Bridgeport, Connecticut. I use the word "job" in quotes above, because in my father's world when he was assigned a task, notably to travel and repair a machine, it was referred to as a job. My older brother Donald had already gone off to college in September of 1953. As I know Don was not at home when Pop returned home with the piece, I consider the fall of 1953 as the earliest possible date.

During the war, Pop was a critical worker who put in long hours. He worked a wartime night shift, often twelve hours each day, plus Saturdays and even some Sundays. His travels as a service representative started after the war, spanning from about 1948 to as late as 1970, at which time his mind and eyesight both started to deteriorate.

He retired from Bullard Machine Tool in 1975 at age 65.

Poster printed by Bullard Machine Tool circa WWII

As Pop traveled, he had an affinity for meeting ordinary working people and offering to buy firearms from whomever might be approachable and willing. Pop felt comfortable around shop people who had "grease under their fingernails." In contrast, anybody who had soft hands (no calluses) and wore a white shirt and a tie was a crook by definition. Pop had disdain for soft people who couldn't put in a day's work. In order to be a man, a man had to show the visible signs of manhood—namely a set of hands with calluses and grease under the fingernails.

Pop's work identification number at Bullard was 171272,

abbreviated as "272." He stamped that number onto his personal tools.

Albert W. Kraus in his wartime Bullard's badge

Pop was employed by Bullard from 1935 to 1975. Over his years of traveling for Bullard's, he brought home close to a dozen firearms. Quality varied widely, but this Walther Model PP made up for the dogs and orphans. Upon returning home, he would remove his haul from the brown leather travel satchel that he used to carry shop manuals, tools, and paperwork. When he brought the Sauckel piece home, it was wrapped in a common shop cloth. Pop placed it onto the kitchen table in front of the family, analogous to how he would throw down a handful of winning cards while playing Pinochle. Pop was one to use gestures as a substitute for language. He placed the pistol on the kitchen table in a wide gesture so as to get our attention.

My memory is somewhat faded, but as I recall, he paid the guy in Ohio $75 for it. Pop was normally not one to say how much he paid for things, be it a boat, car, or firearm. Any discussion of money and how or why it was spent would frequently cause an argument between my parents. My childhood home had its share of arguments, so my mode of operation was to remain silent.

I'm certain that Pop had no knowledge of any special importance of the piece. I also assume that whoever sold it to him in Ohio likewise had no real knowledge of what the piece represented. In the 1950s, paperwork regulations were lax and at times nonexistent as related to the transfer of firearms. This was especially true when the transaction was private and settled in cash. Tight firearm transfer laws didn't come about until the late 1960s when federal laws were enacted in response to the three assassinations (JFK, RFK, and MLK, Jr.) in the mid-1960s.

Another difference about that earlier era was the public's perception of firearms. They were taken for granted, and even displaying a firearm in public was no big deal. I recall that when I was about 14, I often spent a free Saturday with my friend Tommy in the woods near his house. I'd get up bright and early and proceed to walk the several miles to his home. I'd be openly carrying my .22 rifle, and commonly stuck my thumb out to hitch a ride. My most common ride was with the local milkman as he returned from his early morning dairy delivery route. My point is that we live in a vastly different world today. If a 14-year-old kid was seen today carrying a rifle in the open, not to mention hitchhiking, the public would panic. Most likely SWAT teams would be summoned. In all likelihood, the event would make the national news.

Handguns were widespread back then as well. My most common access was some buddy's father or uncle who had left a handgun around, or even in the midst of clutter in the corner of the basement. One day I was surprised to find an antiquated seven shot .22 revolver that took shorts and had a spur trigger. I found this in the garage in a box of metal pieces under my father's work bench. These cheap pistols used to sell for less than $2 in the 1870s and 1880s, and were often referred to as prostitute pistols, as prostitutes would keep one tucked inside their garters. Recall the phrase, "Hotter than a two-dollar pistol." These cheaply made pistols were produced from low quality metals and often exploded when fired.

The pistol I found wasn't complete and didn't even work, but I had access to metal working tools, so I made up the necessary parts so that it would shoot, although barely. A new hammer spring was required, so I made a flat "leaf" spring for the hammer using a piece of a hardened hacksaw blade. In order to shape it, I put the blade in a vise and used a hammer to knock off the excess metal. Then I used a grinding wheel to remove the jagged edges. It worked!

My friend Ned found in his basement a five-shot .32 rimfire, typically made by H&R and Iver Johnson circa the late 1800s. It took us a while to find a box of then 50-year-old .32 short rimfire ammunition, but that pistol was considered utopia to us.

War carrybacks were also common, as often a friend would get his hands on a pistol. After forking out $5 or possibly $25 or so, the pistol was mine. I recall that one was a Belgian-made .25 auto, but it had some missing parts. In contrast, the Walther Model PP in .32 auto was something beyond my wildest of imaginations.

In the fall of 1953, I was 14. As a teenager, I was obsessed with the subject Model PP only because it was a weapon, not because it had any special value other than being shiny and something to shoot, and at times something to carry for my personal protection. My eyes must have been as big as silver dollars when Pop laid that Walther out on the table.

During a later diligent search of the house, I discovered the location of the Walther Model PP, so when urgency required it and I wanted a firearm, this Walther was like a handful of trumps. Recall that I lived in Fairfield, Connecticut, and I lived amongst the children of Mafioso types (as well as other hoodlum street misfits), commonly known to me as punks and hoods. I can recall having the loaded Model PP sitting on the car seat next to me (originally in my 1936 four-door Plymouth sedan, my first car purchased in 1956 for $10). I often used this engraved Walther Model PP as a carry piece from 1955 to 1962.

I still have an affinity for carrying a Model PP or Model PPK, but I now have far greater access to an array of my own firearms, as well as a carry permit. As such, I have upgraded to carry pieces with more stopping power. Nonetheless, the Walther design was then and still remains a classy firearm. The double-action first trigger pull meant that it could be "safely" carried with a live round under the hammer but not cocked. I use quotes on the word "safely" because firearm safety is related to a combination of the individual person's muscle memory, developed habits, and method of handling, in addition to the design features of the firearm.

The $75 price my father paid stands out in my mind for a few reasons. In the years that followed Pop's acquisition of the piece in 1953, and into the 1960s and 1970s, my father and mother kept separate accounts of money and certain other things in their respective lives. Old people do strange things to get along, and my parents were no exception. Each had their own car, allowance money, favorite chair, preferred food, preferred baseball team, separate television sets (little black-and-white sets with rabbit ears), brand loyalties such as which type of gas to put in the car, and so forth. As they did not agree on a number of things, their lives and daily affairs resembled a comedy at times.

I remember that my mother (Ellen M. Kristensen Kraus, 1914-2002) wanted the Sauckel Walther, so she proceeded to take possession of it, being an assertive woman, and in a sense used possession as "nine points." As I recall, my mother merely expropriated the pistol and from that day forth claimed it was hers. My father then became annoyed and complained about his $75.

In order to keep him happy, my mother (so she later told me) paid $75 in restitution to my father in order to terminate his claims to having been cheated out of his money. At that point Pop was focused on what he had paid, and no longer the pistol itself.

Once my mother took control of the Walther, she kept it loaded and tucked away next to her bed. It was her bedside personal defense weapon. Fortunately, she never had a need to fire it.

By the mid-1970s, my father's mental state was deteriorating, and was accompanied by signs of paranoia. Though he suffered from dementia, he still possessed his physical strength and sometimes displayed unpredictable and irrational hostile aggression. So my mother asked me to remove certain weapons from the house. I willingly complied, and that's how I came into possession of the Walther PP. At one point Pop insisted that a certain favorite Luger be returned to him. I did so, but only after having a gunsmith remove the firing pin, rendering it non-firing. When he threatened to shoot a neighbor across the street, we were glad we had taken such precautions.

Of course, one can only speculate as to why the Model PP was sold by the GI in Ohio. My sense is that the then-owner didn't really understand the significance of the piece, or possibly it was his wife that didn't understand the significance. Many wives are concerned about "that gun in the house," especially if there are children around.

Another possibility is that a returning GI was running short of cash and opted to sell the firearm. There is little question in my mind that Pop was at the right place at the right time, and with some expense account cash in his wallet. Yes, in the 1950s a traveling representative for a company would go to the bursar prior to a trip and take out a cash advance. My father dealt in cash and always carried cash.

Although Pop was of direct German and Polish descent, he was strongly American. For example, he forbade the speaking of any foreign languages in our house, because we came to America to be Americans. His father, my grandfather John F. Kraus (1883-1968), immigrated to America in 1900 at age 16 from what is now known as Lithuania, but he was Baltic Deutsch and spoke perfect German.

My father purchased the subject piece because it was a gun, rather than because it had any special historic value or significance. Pop had no interest in its German or Nazi history. His middle name was Wilhelm, which he detested, and so he used the adopted American version "William" instead.

In my father's world, the man of the house was the provider, the person who brought home the bacon. Part of that role as a male provider was to bring things home and yet not discuss money. In short, Albert W. Kraus prided himself (as was evident in his actions, not his words) as one who provided a "roof and three squares." He often derided lesser males who "weren't man enough to buy as much as a quart of milk for their kids, but always had enough money to buy a bottle of whiskey." Even though we lived in a lower-to-middle class working man's neighborhood, as a family we were well-off in comparison to many. We had several cars and a telephone. In contrast, some less fortunate neighborhood families lacked a car, a telephone, as well as amenities we take for granted today, such as an indoor toilet, an electric Frigidaire, and a Maytag wringer washing machine.

My cousin Dorothy lived two doors away. Her family lacked a bathtub as we now know it. Their baths were taken in a galvanized portable tub set on the kitchen floor. The water was heated in kettles on the stove and poured in. It was common for the various family members to reuse the water, each taking a bath in turn.

My Aunt Emma had no washing machine. She did the family laundry using a washing board in the kitchen sink, thus hand scrubbing each garment. As a kid in Fairfield, I recall going to a friend's house and noting that the kitchen cupboard was bare. The family was so poor that they didn't have as much as a spare can of soup in the cupboard. In those days workers were paid weekly, so Friday was known as "payday." Some families ran out of money and food late in the week. Woe to the family if the man of the house stopped at a bar on Friday night, got drunk, and came home without his week's wages.

My father was the strong and silent type who had come up the hard way, working on the docks in Bridgeport and as a laborer during the depression of the 1930s. During my childhood, Pop had a steady-paying job at the factory. He dealt in actions and gestures, not words. Our family never lacked for a roof and warm meals.

Of course, as I now look back, I deeply regret that I didn't ask my father who he purchased the Walther Model PP from. As I mentioned, I was a silent but observant kid. My parents would quarrel over money (and other things as well), and I didn't step into such quarrels. They certainly quarreled over this Walther Model PP. It would have been beyond all possibility that I, a kid, would ask questions about anything Pop brought home. My rule for survival was to remain as silent as possible and preferably out of sight. When Saturday would roll around, my only question was, "Where should I go to get out of here?" My father carried many burdens locked up within him, and my relationship with him was, let me say, distant.

I want to add one additional point regarding my father. Pop did not express any recognition of death or his own dying nor anything else regarding what happens when this life ends. When people died, in his mind it was because they were sick or weak. He, in contrast, willed that he was not sick and not a weakling. As a testament to this, in his four decades of working for Bullard Machine Tool Company, he did not miss a single hour or day of work. He was not sick, late, or absent in 40 years. Family lore says that in the blizzard of '38, Pop walked several miles in deep snow to get to work. Upon arrival, nobody was there as the factory had closed for the day.

If my reader will allow me, I will assert that this very story (which I confess is too long) represents a personal swan song of sorts. I am willing to talk about death and what happens after I pass from this life. My father never would. Along this same line of thinking he would have never thought to write down notes or keep a diary or journal. In contrast, I accept the inevitable that my lips will be cold and silenced someday, but these words will perhaps remain. Pop didn't make any provision for death because he refused to acknowledge even the very existence of death.

Title and Legal Matters

ONCE I BECAME AWARE of the possible value of this Walther around 2001, I asked myself if it would be wise to make public my ownership. One concern was that the family of the original "owner" might be alerted to its existence and then seek its return.

After researching the matter, I learned that the terms of the surrender of Germany and the subsequent occupation stipulated that German nationals were stripped of all rights to own firearms. American soldiers returning with battlefield pick-ups were subject to some paperwork requirements, but I frankly doubt if these requirements were strictly adhered to. The spoils of war were in favor of the winners.

The Question of Valuation

EVEN NOW that I've unraveled some of the mysteries surrounding the Sauckel piece (except for absolute confirmation of the recipient), it is hard to place a valuation on the piece. I have standing offers from two prominent militaria collectors (one collector made his offer sight unseen!), each in the low five-figures. There are few comparable sales or appraisals. Pieces of this rarity are seldom traded, and instead often remain in museums or private collections. While other engraved handguns exist, the number with engraved signatures of historically prominent persons is small.

Factory-engraved Walther presentation pistols were typically produced in batches with consecutive serial numbers. A similar pistol to the subject Walther was presented to Ante Pavelic, the Nazi leader of Croatia. Its serial number, 109815P, is just 10 numbers prior to the Fritz Sauckel pistol. This firearm has an emblem on the front ivory grip with the engraved initials A.P., but does not have a donor signature inscription. Ante Pavelic led the brutal regime that was responsible for the mass murder of several hundred thousand Serbs and tens of thousands of Jews and Romanians living in Croatia during the war. At the end of the war in 1945, he fled to Austria and eventually made his way to

Argentina. In 1957, he was wounded in an assassination attempt and died from his wounds in 1959. Although significant, this pistol's history doesn't compare to the evil associated with the subject Fritz Sauckel Walther PP.

Military items, especially from the Third Reich with a Nazi connection, are bringing what can best be described as substantial prices. A signed photo of Wilhelm von Brückner was recently listed at $1,200. A pair of collar insignia for the rank of General was listed on a Florida-based website for $3,000.

As to the matter of condition, the subject Sauckel Walther Model PP is in fair to good condition as compared to other presentation pieces where photos are available. It still has the original magazine, but only the one with flat (or flush) bottom. The customary magazine with curved finger extension is missing. There is no presentation box. The grips are in good condition with no visible cracks and only minimal discoloration. There is evidence of some rusting under the nickel plate, but considering the history, this piece is in reasonable condition.

I note that other prominent Nazis had similar plated Model PP's with oak leaf scroll engraving, some of which were given over during the formal surrender. I read years ago in *Time Magazine* [14] of one such surrendered Model PP, that of SS General Karl Wolff and bearing Himmler's signature as donor, on display in the U.S. Army Museum at West Point.

A recent Internet search revealed that several Sauckel Walther Model PP presentation pieces have sold in five figures. As a comparable firearm, the Eva Braun engraved Model PP was valued by Rock Island Auction Company in the range of $30,000 to $50,000. Rock Island Auction, Lot #3674 listed a PPK that sold for $28,750 circa 2007. Rock Island Auction Lot #3641, also an engraved Sauckel piece, sold at auction for $25,875. One sale in 2013 brought $43,000. Some of these presentation pieces were in lesser condition and did not have a recipient's medallion on the ivory grip.

Deadly Bribe

I found a website in Russian that depicted a Sauckel presentation piece engraved to Wilhelm Keppler (1882-1960), Nazi supporter and financier. Note that immediately under the inscription to Wilhelm Keppler is the engraved signature of Fritz Sauckel. Just to the right of Sauckel's signature the dedication reads "zum 55 Geburtstag" meaning given in honor of Keppler's 55th birthday, so I deduce it was given on or about December 14, 1937. The website, complete with photographs, places the starting bid at 13,500 Euros (just under $19,000 USD).

Wilhelm Keppler Walther Model PP presentation pistol

The above photograph shows the Keppler Walther Model PP. The serial number is 989508, thus suggesting a different production scheduling from the Sauckel pistol. Both this Keppler Model PP and the subject "W.B." Walther PP in my possession have what I will describe as the 60-degree safety lever, thus different than the Fritz Sauckel piece (with a 90-degree lever) shown in an earlier photograph.

This piece is in some ways similar but in other ways dissimilar to the subject Model PP. This specimen's condition is more deteriorated. The *Wilhelm Gustloff Stiftung* is shown on the medallion as opposed to being engraved into the piece. The ivory grips show cracks and discoloration. One significant positive is that the recipient's identity is clearly established.

The fascination of Americans with the American Wild West heritage is strong. Demand for firearms only increases when they can be associated with persons from the old west—on whatever side of the law they fell. The desire for Nazi-era firearms is also strong, but possibly not as strong as the desire to own a piece of the American Wild West. A Colt Single Action Army (SAA) firearm attributed to the Wild West Dalton Gang recently sold (according to an Internet source) for a price in excess of $150,000. Another example is the Colt SAA carried by Texas Ranger Captain Frank Hamer, who tracked down famed bank robbers Bonnie and Clyde in 1934, which sold for $178,250. Yes, when firearms can be associated with (in)famous people and events, their prices rise.

Movies and our culture as well have had impacts. For example, the non-firing James Bond PPK (de-commissioned due to the UK's strict gun laws) used in the movie *Goldfinger* fetched at auction a price in the vicinity of $101,000. The Bond Model PP used in *Doctor No* brought $106,000 at auction. Interestingly, the *Doctor No* script called for a PPK, but due to a mix-up the scene was shot using a PP. Few movie viewers recognized the mistaken use of a PP. Other Bond 007 movie props (non-firearm related) have ranged from $10,000 to $50,000 and upwards at various auctions. Again, the various Bond artifacts are non-functioning movie props. The Bond firearms, being de-commissioned, attain their value because of the one-time use and association to a fictional movie character, and in no way have any history other than as movie images. The hat used by Odd Job in *Goldfinger* is reported to have brought $134,750 at a recent auction. Obviously, there is a mania for investors to buy and hold James Bond 007 artifacts and memorabilia. This website [15] lists various James Bond memorabilia.

Firearms with comparable histories to the subject Sauckel Presentation Walther Model PP rarely surface and even more rarely are traded. The U.S. Army Museum at West Point has an engraved Nazi era pistol attributed to Nazi General Karl Wolff, the Nazi commander of occupied Italy. A second Walther Model PP, also attributed to General Wolff, was auctioned off by the Rock Island Auction. The estimated price prior to auction was between $90,000 and $160,000. But when the auction gavel fell, the sale price was astonishingly slightly over $250,000.

I feel compelled to contrast the Wolff pistol and the Sauckel presentation pistol. The Wolff pistol was associated with a German general. There was no reference to any date or event of significance. The Wolff pistol was accompanied by documentation of the American who found the pistol under the pillow in Wolff's quarters in Italy after Wolf was in Allied custody.

The Fritz Sauckel engraved subject pistol has certain attributes that add to its significance and value. The donor signed and dated the gift on behalf of the Wilhelm Gustloff Stiflung. Hitler is documented to have been in attendance at its presentation. One notable person associated with the piece, although not present, is Winston Churchill. The date is closely tied to the events of Kristallnacht—a planned and horrific happening that was used to justify the Holocaust, thus causing six million Jews to be exterminated. The donor, Fritz Sauckel, lowlife that he was, hid in a network of caves to escape. At his trial, Sauckel never showed the slightest remorse for his actions. All these attributes give the subject pistol a significant place in World War II history.

Shakespeare pondered, "Is it the bee that stings; or is it the bee's wax that stings?" The point is that legal rulings are vastly more deadly than mere bullets fired from a weapon. In the case of this Sauckel Walther Presentation Pistol, assume for the sake of discussion that Walter Buch was the recipient. Given that assumption, it was a deadly bribe. The bribe resulted in the genocide of millions.

In my mind, there is no comparison between the two pistols. What remains is for some future historian to advance the research and documentation.

I am aware that some people will forever resent the Holocaust and thus want any and all Nazi-era memorabilia vaporized. My belief is that such memorabilia are spoils of war, and stand as monuments to our form of government, ideals, and economic way of life. I am also a capitalist, as I believe in the free market. War trophy pieces are worth however much or little willing buyers and sellers might determine.

In my case, I have no intention of ever selling this piece. I certainly won't allow it to be melted down and become a manhole cover in Detroit. I have spent considerable time digging up and researching its history, mostly to serve as a gift to my children and grandchildren and to our community at large. History, in my view, must be preserved and taught.

If we as a society would opt to vaporize all things with a Nazi background, we would be in a sore state. I will cite several illustrations to support my point:

The Eisenhower Interstate Highway System was modeled directly on the German Autobahns, one of Hitler's public works endeavors. Eisenhower was amazed at how rapidly the Germans using the Autobahns could move men and equipment throughout and about Germany to bring up reserves as needed.

When we use our GPS devices, they rely on the marvels of space exploration, namely earth-orbiting satellites. Our dominance in space is a direct consequence of the fact that our Germans were better than the Germans who defected to the Soviet side.

What we call the "jerry can," used for transport of fuel, was a German invention. Our side needed a similar can for fuel transport. Our military was able to capture some early jerry cans and base our production by copying the German design.

As I listen to the inner bells that ring within my mind, my

view is that Nazi-era memorabilia, especially these rare Sauckel presentation pieces, are undervalued. I recently attended a gun show in Belleville, Illinois, where to my amazement a Nazi cloth cap was offered for sale at $2,000. I have seen Nazi flags in the asking range of up to $5,000. With all that said, I am confident that real Sauckel Gustloff Walthers are presently undervalued when compared to Hollywood stage props or Single Action Army "peacemaker" Colts from the late 1800s and early 1900s with no tie to any particular famous historical figure or historical event.

Authentication from Letters and Factory Records

AUTHENTICATION, of course, is yet another issue, as throughout history fakes have surfaced or been alleged. In my case, I have had personal knowledge of the piece and its ownership continually since 1953, thus over 67 years. I accept the story of how it came into my father's possession beyond question. The serial numbering as well as proof marks are all consistent with the period. The piece is my property, and I have no intention of liquidating it.

Firearms of collector grade that are allegedly tied to famous people often require extensive paper documentation to support valuation. As an example, I recall seeing at the Tulsa Gun Show a Smith & Wesson .38SPL revolver that Elvis Presley had given to a household employee along with a signed letter by Elvis wherein he acknowledged the gift. In that case, the asking price was in five figures but the firearm itself had no special markings beyond the letter itself to indicate any tie to Elvis.

In some special cases, the firearm constitutes its own certification or pedigree, thus somewhat negating the need for supporting paper documentation. Such is the case with this Sauckel Model PP presentation piece. The engraved signature on the piece documents the donor, Fritz Sauckel, a notorious war criminal. The date of the donation is well documented, again by the inscription on the piece. Historic events, all documented, coincide and authenticate the date and circumstances of the presentation. The only remaining significant uncertainty is the confirmation of the recipient.

Even if the identity of the recipient is never resolved, this piece is still associated with incredibly important events and people. The Gautag's date of November 5-6, 1938 agrees with the date inscribed on the Model PP. Hitler's presence in Weimar on that date is solid and beyond argument, as Hitler gave his speech denouncing Churchill in Weimar on that date. The recipient's initials "W.B." are on the presentation piece. Based on comparable Sauckel presentation pieces, the elegance of the medallion with initials distinguishes this piece above most. The 1938 Weimar Gautag represents the zenith of the rise of the Third Reich. By inference, the recipient was a pinnacle Nazi of great importance. I argue that the recipient was someone singled out by Sauckel for the honor so bestowed. Sauckel, by his presence, represents the *Wilhelm Gustloff Stiftung*, the donor. All these details dovetail to complete the picture. Sufficient numbers of other Sauckel presentation PP's exist to provide benchmarks as to the authenticity.

When the issue of the recipient is resolved, the valuation will only increase. Please bear in mind however that the candidate list is by no means complete. Other recipients yet to be identified must be investigated as well. The short list comprising Buch, Buhle, and Brauchitsch contains Nazis of high stature. Any future valuation would be impacted as such.

In this book I have argued the case that Walter Buch was the recipient. Upon definite establishment of the Buch and Kristallnacht connection, the historical importance and desirability will escalate. The Holocaust took an estimated six million Jewish lives. Buch's court ruling was foundational to the entire Holocaust. Assuming my hypothesis is confirmed, I challenge anyone to identify a comparable firearm with as much historical significance.

The month of November was especially significant to the Nazi heritage. The 1923 Munich Beer Hall Putsch took place in November. The humiliating German surrender in The Great War was signed in November 1918. For the Nazi Third Reich, November was sort of like Christmas, Easter, and the Fourth of July all wrapped up into one. In addition, the year 1938 was the crest of the rise of the Third Reich as Hitler prepared for the aggressions of WWII. Hitler was tightening his grip on nearby territories and casting his eyes onto Austria and Czechoslovakia.

November 1938 in Germany was also a busy time as the infamous *Kristallnacht* or "the night of broken glass" followed within a few days of the Gautag, on the night of November 9-10, 1938. On that night throughout Germany, nearly 100 Jews were murdered, hundreds of Jewish-owned businesses and synagogues were smashed and looted, Jewish cemeteries were vandalized, and around 30,000 to 50,000 Jews were rounded up for deportation to concentration camps. These events and this period of time approach historic proportion. I also submit that *Kristallnacht* did not appear out of nowhere. Most certainly it was a planned and staged event, so obviously the plans were firm, known, disseminated, and discussed at the time of the Weimar Gautag just days before.

Even though I say the piece is not for sale, in reality there is a price for which virtually anything (tangible) is for sale. I am at an age and point in my life where money is not my immediate concern. I struggle knowing that our society at large deserves to have access to this Sauckel Walther presentation piece. Additional research needs to be conducted. I am ready to pass on the baton to others more qualified than me. The future could well include display in a reputable museum. As an example, the National Rifle Association museum in Fairfax, Virginia, comes to mind.

Ask yourself this question: "How many times in your lifetime have you had the opportunity to handle a firearm attributed to so much history—especially the history of one where the donor (and obvious owner at one point) has been proven without any doubt to have been a notorious criminal responsible for the deaths of hundreds of thousands of innocents, and who was then caught while hiding as a fugitive, tried and pronounced guilty, protested with indignation his pending execution, and hanged in a botched manner by the neck until dead?" All in all, this firearm has been tied to events in history that dwarf the events surrounding all but very few other firearms. To top this, the likelihood of Walter Buch being the next-in-line owner brings the evil associated with this firearm potentially to even greater proportions. Instead of hundreds of thousands, we are now discussing numbers as high as ten million people executed.

On a personal note, my search for the history of this firearm now spans six decades. For years, I had set aside the firearm as I had higher priorities. As I entered into retirement in the late 1990s, I finally had the time to devote to research. Two events triggered the breakthrough. The first was a spur of the moment idea around 1999 to show the piece to the membership of a local gun rights organization. A member and close friend, knowledgeable in firearms, recognized the engraved signature as that of Fritz Sauckel. The second factor spurring the research was my increasing Internet search proficiency.

To me, the Walther Model PP is akin to the theme of *The Sorcerer's Apprentice*. Whenever one question is asked, instead of getting an answer one often gets two more questions. The number of unanswered questions is almost boundless. I also must confess that I have become intensely attracted to the research, and by inference, Nazi-era history. The intrigue is almost beyond description. If I were to attempt to write a fictional story, it would be overshadowed by the true events that surround this piece.

Postscript

MY PURPOSE IN WRITING is to document my research on the Sauckel Walther so that my children who will inherit the piece will benefit from it. I have built a staging ground for an assault on uncharted territory. The future is waiting to be grasped. This story isn't complete; the final chapters remain to be written. As I write, my eyesight is failing. Yet, I am not a complainer. My heart leaps for joy as I ponder the future.

I want to add some summary remarks based on my thoughts as of late.

I try to imagine the stories that would come out if this Model PP could talk—about the things, people, and events of its eight decades of existence. Being a piece of metal, it can't talk, but in truth it can. The piece tells its story with its own documentation, based on the inscriptions, serial number, engraving, WWII archives, etc.

With the advent of the Internet, I've been able to uncover an incredible amount of information. Large files of WWII documents and history have been compiled, and these have been made available in electronic form, allowing Internet search engines to ferret out all sorts of details. Even just four decades ago, it would have been unthinkable to do the type of research that I have been able to do.

We have only scratched the surface in terms of what is still waiting out there. Throughout the Nazi era, Hitler and his cronies had professional photographers take pictures of nearly everything. Heinrich Hoffmann stands center front. These photographs documenting the Third Reich still exist to a great extent, tens upon tens of thousands of them. I am confident that a day will come when photos or other evidence surface of this Sauckel Walther piece being presented by Fritz Sauckel. We will recognize it because the date, city, and people present will be recorded. With high certainty, we know the piece was given in the city of Weimar, obviously presented by Sauckel, and the date coincides with the date of the inscription, November 5-6, 1938. We have proof that Hitler and Sauckel were in Weimar on that date, as per photos, printed newspaper accounts, and Hitler's speech which rebutted Churchill. Because Hitler was in Weimar on that date, it is highly plausible that photographers were there as well. As said previously, the photos survived the war and many (I have read of numbers as high as 85,000) are available in public archives.

This Walther Sauckel PP is unique, even to the point of being museum grade. I feel that its history should be made available to collectors and to military historians. Just as I am searching for related pieces to help solve the puzzle, or to fit the pieces together, it only stands to reason that other collectors and even curators are searching for the knowledge represented by what I hold. Accordingly, I feel that it is in fact an obligation on my part to make public the existence of this pistol and its story as I have been best able to fit the pieces together.

As the present owner of the pistol, I am willing to share, but sharing does not mean relinquishing total control. My past experiences with museums have been, quite frankly, disappointing at best. In one instance, a set of surgeon's tools dating from the late 1800s and the horse-and-buggy country doctor's days simply vanished. The museum curator had no explanation and even less concern.

As I weigh these matters, I will examine my options. I will say that if I am able at some time in the future to entice a reputable museum into accepting this piece on loan, that acceptance would help establish its authenticity. Moreover, many military firearms collectors are available who at some point can weigh in, and at that time my amateurish thrusts and musings will cede way.

Yes, I have included many facts and citations from the Internet, as well as downloaded photographs. Obviously, statements and photographs from Internet sources are not completely reliable and are thus error prone, however I have opted to include them to fill out the larger picture. Any errors (of which there may be many) are not intended and in no way detract from the overall story as I attempt to unravel the mystery of this subject Walther Model PP. This was done as an expediency, but bear in mind that I cite and make clear such practices. As time marches on, the errors will inevitably be caught and corrected or filtered out. Said another way, I feel that the benefits of including unverified Internet sources outweigh the risks as I attempt to give my reader the broader story of this Walther Model PP.

I am not fluent in the German language, so that puts me at a distinct disadvantage. A trip to visit archives in Germany might be a possibility, but the cost-benefit is hard for me to justify. In contrast, the Internet and a search of sources within the U.S. seem to be more prudent options. I do enjoy showing the piece, so I might set up a display at a prominent gun show one day, perhaps the Indy 1500 Gun and Knife Show or the massive Wanenmacher Gun Show in Tulsa.

In regard to the history of WWII, I have enjoyed reading the entire six-volume set by Churchill published after the war. Churchill made two observations early on: one as the war approached and one in the early phases of the *blitzkrieg*. His first observation was that all wars are required to be named. In the mid-

1930s Churchill felt that the most appropriate name would be *The Unnecessary War*. Churchill lamented that if in 1936 France and the U.K. had held Hitler to the line so as to prevent his early expansions, the war would not have occurred. Hence the name: *The Unnecessary War*.

Churchill's second observation concerned the *blitzkrieg*. Although tanks and similar armored vehicles can move in fast and occupy town squares, without the support of ground troops (which necessarily move far more slowly and are themselves dependent upon support which moves slowly as well) the tank's presence ceases to be a threat. After several days, the crew inside the tank will require supplies including food and water. Upon emerging from the tank to seek these necessary basics, the tank crew is easily dealt with by a few snipers (even citizens) with high powered rifles. In communications to the French government in 1940 prior to the fall of France, Churchill implored the French to not capitulate just because some armored vehicles had entered France.

Churchill clearly understood the vital need for free people to be armed. As an aside, the Second Amendment does not grant us as citizens the right to keep and bear arms, but rather affirms rights already in place. For example, the Magna Carta in 1215 enumerates such rights.

Of all the photographs reprinted within this book, perhaps the one with the greatest impact on me is the crowded street scene at the 1938 Weimar Gautag with tens of thousands gathered to hear Hitler's speech. The pomp and ceremony of those present acclaiming the glory of the Third Reich suggests that this honorary Walther would not have been given to some obscure unknown "Willie von Broom-pusher," but rather to someone of considerable stature.

APPENDIX A: Serial Numbers of Factory Engraved Walthers

THE INFORMATION IN THIS APPENDIX was provided by Tom Whiteman, an expert in collectible military weapons, particularly engraved pistols.

Walther PP's and PPK's intended for presentation were factory engraved in batches within a consecutive range of serial numbers [16]. A pattern of oak leaf and acorns was the most common engraving, but many examples have a vine/floral pattern.

Production of engraved pistols stopped in 1941 or 1942, but was resumed in 1944 by Heinrich Himmler. Post-1944 engraved PP's are much more common.

Below is a list of serial number ranges for the rarer pre-1944 PP's and PPK's, along with the year in which they were manufactured:

PPK's
1002878 - 1002923 (1938)
202879K - 202893K (1938)
210961K - 211017K (1939)
230015K - 230055K (1939)
261437K - 261491K (1940)
314134K - 314150K (1941)
408106K - 408148K (1944)

PP's
961623 - 961680 (1937)
972851 - 972871 (1938)
976421 - 976587 (1938)
989457 - 989524 (1938)

109806P - 109841P (1938-1939)
127443P - 127675P (1939)
139762P - 139802P (1939)
162703P - 162810P (1940)
192884P - 192977P (1940)
215153P - 215934P (1940)
293008P - 293995P (1942)

Occasionally, the factory received an unplanned special request from a high-ranking party official for an engraved PP or PPK, so sometimes there are one-offs not within the serial number ranges above.

Fritz Sauckel probably ordered and gave out 12-20 engraved PP's. Following is a list of the serial numbers of known Sauckel presentation PP's, all gold engraved with ivory grips:

763834 - 1933
961631 - 1937
961652 - 1937
976437 - 1937
976487 - 1937
989524 - 1937/38, given to William Keppler
109825 - 1938
109841 - 1938
122051 - 1938/39

Perhaps in the future, more of them will turn up and be positively identified.

APPENDIX B: The Author's Affinity for Firearms

Here are some of the reasons I enjoy owning and collecting firearms:
- Firearms as tools are functional. They permit one to perform tasks.
- They are historic. Firearms reveal the story of civilization and the advance of mankind.
- They recount human creativity and technical advances. The development of firearms mirrors the development of industrialization. They spearheaded mankind's rise and rebuke of enslavement and tyranny. I am reminded of the famous quotation, "God made all men, but Sam Colt made all men equal."
- They provide tangible remedies should a crisis arise; remedies that are vastly faster and more effective than dialing 9-1-1.
- They're social. As a gun aficionado, one can discern who is friend and who is foe. For example, I know I am among friends when at the range or a gun show.
- They simplify daily affairs. In a complex world filled with political agendas, I can easily spot pandering politicians. Support of the Second Amendment is easy to rattle off, such as "I support your right to go rabbit-hunting." Language is the key to identifying the pretender. Do they know the difference between a magazine and a clip? What is the difference between semi and full auto? What is the significance of a yellow shotgun shell? Why do certain handguns eject spent casings, but not all handguns? What characterizes a rimfire from a centerfire? What is meant by FMJ? What is the origin

of the expression, "Give 'em the whole nine yards"? What is a 4473? Just who was Heller, and why do we care? The firearms vocabulary is both complex and precise. Improper language usage is the key to spotting wolves in sheep's clothing, and sensing a true friend from foe.

- They are intergenerational. I can connect with grandchildren by getting handguns out or going to the shooting range.
- They are a means of storing wealth. Politicians can print paper money and debase wealth represented by paper documents, but firearms as physical objects are difficult to debase.
- Firearms as an investment rarely achieve zero value. Even in the worst of condition, they are still worth something, typically $100. This applies broadly as "buy back" programs pay a reward for anything resembling a firearm. Even those missing internal parts, having cracked barrels, rusted , or fire destroyed still qualify. Personally, I smile broadly getting paid good dollars for worthless junk.
- They are movable, easily hidden, and compact. Unlike bank deposits, stocks, bonds, and even real estate, few public records exist identifying gun ownership and the wealth represented.
- As the anti-gun crowd attacks gun ownership, firearms rise in value.
- Weapons are universally recognized as barter—physical objects that can be traded.
- When properly selected and cared for, they represent good investments. Firearms from quality manufacturers tend to hold their value and even increase in value.
- Transactions between private persons tend to be nondocumented and free of taxation. Firearms are commonly bought and sold for cash. Those in the gun culture both like and respect privacy. Paper trails are few and can easily be circumvented. Also, the spread between buy and sell is small and often nonexistent.
- Their values endure, even enduring revolutions, fiat currency

inflations, and the collapses of governments.
- The value of a firearm is determined between buyer and seller. As a non-quoted market, the skilled trader can benefit from shrewd trading skills.
- They are fun, like toys, a delight to handle. In contrast, few persons take delight in handling stocks, bonds, and paper certificates.
- They are sporting in nature. As Jefferson noted, the sport develops the mind in addition to the body.
- They shape human behaviors. Instruction in shooting encourages young minds to become proactive and self-confident.
- They are foundational for building critical life and survival skills. Being proficient in marksmanship is accompanied by increased survival and self-defense skills, notably situational awareness and early recognition of predatory behavior.
- Firearms provide a platform for creativity. Akin to Legos®, bits and pieces can be creatively assembled. Modern firearms, typified by the AR lower platform, can be designed and assembled in near limitless configurations.
- The sport of shooting is available to virtually all, independent of age and physical limitations.
- Owning firearms allows the ownership to irritate the daylights out of the gun-haters.

A Note from the Author

Dear Reader,

Thank you for taking the time to read this book, *Deadly Bribe*. I've been in possession of the subject Walther Sauckel PP presentation piece for 67 years and counting. Now, as an 80-something-year-old retiree, I finally had the time to publish my research from the past 40 years. I am convinced that few other firearms hold as much history as this piece, and I am glad to have shared this piece's story with you.

I trust you have enjoyed reading *Deadly Bribe*. If so, I'd appreciate it if you left a review on Amazon. Reviews help other readers decide to try out a new book. Just a sentence or two saying what you liked about the book will do!

Thanks again for reading and for helping get this book into the hands of other readers.

Blessings,
Rudolf E. Kraus

About the Author

Rudolf E. "Rudy" Kraus was born at the end of the Great Economic Depression. He was raised in Fairfield, Connecticut. Rudy has strong recollections of the closing years of World War II, as this was when he was impacted by the massive national mobilization required to win the war and for America to emerge victorious.

Following his high school years, Rudy worked in automobile repair. As computers and the information age emerged, Rudy tired of bruised knuckles and thus shifted to computer programming and information technology. Rudy also became interested in shooting sports, hunting, gun smithing work, and collecting both antique and modern firearms.

As a firearms aficionado, and because of the need to maintain a low profile, Rudy elects to remain in the shadows as opposed to becoming an obvious target.

For hobbies, Rudy enjoys country music and reading biographies of famous and successful technically inclined people. He also has a strong interest in World War II history. Rudy, in the footsteps of Hemingway, has accomplished four goals in life: planting a tree, fathering a son, writing a book, and fighting a bull. What else could possibly remain undone?

Rudy can be contacted at the following address:
Rudolf E. Kraus
c/o Great Banyan Press
1480 Pearl Street
Alton, IL 62002

Acknowledgments

Acknowledgment is due to four individuals. People who own and bear firearms tend to hang low, below the radar screen. Quite frankly, they prefer to remain in the shadows. In order to recognize the first three individuals and yet respect their privacy, I will call them merely Peter, Paul, and Perry.

I credit Peter for being the person who first recognized the signature of Fritz Sauckel. I also credit him for additional leads, research, and contacts.

Paul, a noted Third Reich collector, has personally inspected the piece and was sufficiently persuaded of its authenticity that he has made a standing offer in five figures to purchase it. Paul is in possession of a similar engraved Sauckel piece, but in lesser condition, and the two pieces laid side-by-side confirm the signature, style of engraving of the oak leaf scroll, and the recipient's medallion.

At a family wedding in November 2013, I was thrilled to meet an unusual person, Perry. He was born in Germany the same year as me, 1939. Perry came to America in the early 1960s. In my conversations with Perry, he has shared vivid memories of life in Germany as a child during WWII and the aftermath. For example, he told me of his mother's successful efforts to hide from the Allies certain contraband, notably his father's WWII German uniform. According to Perry, his mother wrapped the uniform in sackcloth and suspended it within the chimney of the house. The Allies never found it. Without too much elaboration, Perry implied that he and his mother parted ways. He came to America seeking a better life. His mother remained a diehard Nazi, still hoping for the Third Reich to rebound and to rule the Earth. Some people never give up.

I would also like to acknowledge Tom Whiteman, the President of Legacy Collectibles, located in Pennsylvania. I regard Tom as perhaps the world's foremost authority on engraved Nazi era firearms. He rendered invaluable advice and commentary during the writing of this book and reviewed the text before publishing. I extend a heartfelt thanks to Tom for all his help.

As I have stated, this story is not over. More research remains to be done. For anyone looking to pick up the baton, Perry has two suggestions:

1) Contact the German Military Research Institute for more information. Their address is:

> Militaergeschichliches Forschungsami
> Gruenwaelderstrasse 1 – 14
> Freiburg i. Breisgau 7800, Germany

2) Contact the National Archives, as it contains thousands of documents, artifacts, photographs, films, and personal items of prominent Nazi members. I must add that Perry has a deep knowledge of WWII history, including engagements, the people, firearms, and armaments.

Table of Illustrations

The Fritz Sauckel Presentation Walther, view of engraved side . 5
The Wilhelm Gustloff Stiftung engraving 6
The Fritz Sauckel engraving 6
The Fritz Sauckel Presentation Walther with Crown N proof mark and serial number 7
The engraved initials of the recipient on the ivory grip 8
The engraved flush bottom of the magazine 10
View of factory name, Walther Zella-Mehlis 11
The most common photograph of Ernst "Fritz" Sauckel 16
Fritz Sauckel (1894-1946) 17
Sauckel's personal pistol 18
Gustloff assassination Nazi propaganda poster 20
The M.S. Wilhelm Gustloff painted white as a hospital ship 21
The sinking of the M.S. Wilhelm Gustloff 23
Administrative map of the Third Reich 25
Bunker 0 of underground Gustloff Werke factory at Weimar . 28
Final aircraft assembly 27
Artist's conception of the completed Gauforum 29
Groundbreaking for the Gauforum May 1, 1937 29
Massive crowds at groundbreaking of Gauforum site 30
Hitler speaking at the 1938 Weimar Gautag 32
Postcard from 1938 Weimar Gautag 31
Hitler at Haus Elephant in 1936 35
Hitler at the balcony of Haus Elephant in November 1938 36
Weimar Gautag tinnie with incorrect date 38
Hitler and his entourage in Weimar at the 1938 Gautag 33
Bunkers near Weimar 42
Sauckel and seven co-defendants at the Nuremberg trials 44

Sauckel's body after pronouncement of death....................45
Werner Best (1903-1989) 48
Brauchitsch with Hitler in Warsaw, October 1939..................50
Wilhelm von Brückner (1884-1954) 52
Brückner with white military uniform. 53
Walther von Brauchitsch (1881-1948) 67
Walther von Brauchitsch on the cover of Time magazine........69
Walther Buhle...71
Walter Buch (1883-1949)..72
Hitler's general staff, June 1940....................................77
Poster printed by Bullard Machine Tool circa WWII 86
Albert W. Kraus in his wartime Bullard's badge...................87
Wilhelm Keppler Walther Model PP presentation pistol...........99

References

1. Wistrick, Robert S., *Who's Who in Nazi Germany*, Weidenfeld & Nicolson, 1982. Reprinted by Routledge, 1995.
2. Bennet Schulte / Wikimedia Commons / CC BY-SA 4.0. <https://commons.wikimedia.org/w/index.php?curid=62154983>
3. Bundesarchiv, Bild 141-2738 / CC-BY-SA 3.0 / CC BY-SA 3.0 DE. <https://creativecommons.org/licenses/by-sa/3.0/de/deed.en>
4. Shirer, William L., Berlin Diary 1934-1941: The Rise of the Third Reich, p. 196.
5. From the collection of Dr. Klaus Magdlung, created by his uncle Karl Magdlung in the 1940s. <http://www.weimar-historischefotos.de/weimarfotos/strassen/Gauforum/pages/K2-342_2.html>
6. Kirsten, Holm, Weimar im Banne des Führers: die Besuche Adolf Hitlers 1925-1940, Böhlau, 2001, ISBN 3412031011, 9783412031015.
7. "Hitler's Weimar Speech of November 6, 1938". Our Legacy of Truth. <https://www.stormfront.org/posterity/ns/11-6-8.html>
8. Bundesarchiv, Bild 183-R99057 / Unknown / CC-BY-SA 3.0, CC BY-SA 3.0 de. <https://commons.wikimedia.org/w/index.php?curid=5368831>
9. Public domain. <https://commons.wikimedia.org/wiki/File:Nuremberg-1-.jpg>
10. Public domain. <http://commons.wikimedia.org/wiki/File:Dead_fritzsauckel.jpg>
11. Infield, Glenn B., *Secrets of the SS*, Military Heritage Press, 1982.
12. Bundesarchiv, Bild 146-1978-127-21 / CC-BY-SA 3.0, CC BY-SA 3.0 de. <https://commons.wikimedia.org/w/

index.php?curid=5482975>
13. Hart, B. H. Liddell, *The German Generals Talk*, Quill, New York, 1979.
14. *Time Magazine*, October 6, 1967, p. 86-89.
15. Debord, Jason (April 12, 2008). "Ian Fleming's 'James Bond' Letters Fetch Nearly $30,000 at Auction", Original Prop Blog. <https://www.originalprop.com/blog/?p=2117>
16. Legacy Collectibles, Paoli, PA. Mr. Tom Whiteman, President.

Made in the USA
Coppell, TX
23 March 2021